S IN ICKNESS AND IN H EALTH

IN
SICKNESS
AND IN
HEALTH

TERRY ATKINSON

NEW LIVING PUBLISHERS
164 Radcliffe New Road, Whitefield, Manchester M45 7TU
England

British Library Cataloguing in Publication Data
A catalogue record for this book is available
from the British Library.

ISBN 1 899721 01 0

The King James version of the Bible is used throughout,
unless otherwise stated.
The N.I.V. is the New International Version;
R.S.V. the Revised Standard Version;
A.S.V. the Authorised Standard Version.

Produced and printed in England for
NEW LIVING PUBLISHERS
164 Radcliffe New Road, Whitefield, Manchester M45 7TU by
Nuprint Ltd, Station Road, Harpenden, Herts, AL5 4SE

Contents

Preface

*I*n *Sickness And In Health* is not simply or thoroughly a book
about sickness. It is a book more about suffering than sickness,
and there is a subtle difference. It deals with sickness, but also
with trouble, burdens, trials, difficulties, that which has been pained
and hurt, and a number of other key issues which we all experience
in the Christian Life. It is a book for Christians, and it opens up the
hidden pains we sometimes have to bear. Commencing with sickness, we are left with the many avenues of healing, not only of sickness, but depression, misunderstanding, hurt and pain. There is a
salve here for every malady.

Commencing in the Introduction, with the different suggestions as
to how we can be healed, we then move on swiftly into another
theme, that of sickness, and the many questions it presents. Little by
little the picture of the Christian, the many moods, the many disappointments, the many challenges are revealed, discussed, and met
with by faith in Jesus Christ. The back is never turned upon them,
and there is no pretense that they are not there. This book is written
for the Christian Believer, to help each one in and with their struggles
until glory appears, and they treat their light affliction as it should be
treated, as a tool, rather than as burden or limitation. If that nature
of Christ is going to be developed in each disciple, then we must
expect God to use all our circumstances to influence us, and bring us
unto and into glory. The glory of the new birth, the glory of the new
nature, the glory of trusting and going through rather than succumb-
ing to any and every temptation. The glory of His care. The glory of
His understanding. The glory of His provision. Let the strong winds
blow, but they will never blow away that which is born of faith.

Moving from chapter to chapter, we are confronted with patience,
sorrow and loneliness. Weaknesses are met and dealt with as new
strength is found. The suffering Servant is seen in Jesus Christ.
Grace and glory are found side by side. Bruising and blessing are
part of life, and these are fully developed.

Whatever enrichment we pass through, there will be times when we wish we had a man to represent how we feel before God. The patience of Job leads to that man requesting a Daysman, who might stand before God for him. We seek to understand how the patriarch finds such a One, and how we may find one who is touched with the feelings of our infirmities. The next portion, after we have met with the Man of Sorrows, is to find and receive grace from that Man, Jesus Christ. This book is all about the discovering of grace and how great that grace can be in every surrounding. Jesus Christ is the one revealed not only as one associated with our sorrows, but One who suffered as we do. This brings a sense of oneness in every dilemma. Jesus has been here! The availability of God is always assured, and through it, every portion of suffering is only there to meet a need, and to complete a work. The chaff goes while the real corn remains. Pain is sanctified by His presence. Promises are ratified by His power.

Chapter seven reveals the believer as a smouldering wick, which is not put out. This brings to us a sense of the gentleness of God which follows the grace of God. When we are almost ready to lose faith, and even die, then He comes to pour in the oil and the wine. He gently blows upon the dying embers. God is a Carer, and he is seen as such in the next chapter. The bruised reed he does not break. Whatever we have gone through, whatever has been our failing, this God comes to revive us, and bring that back into a life which has long since disappeared. He never bruises to breaking, but to making. This is all about character.

Chapter nine leads into the loneliness which we can feel when we are suffering from sickness or carrying a burden. We do have worrying times. When the problem seems as much part of us as the tail seems to the dog or its tongue, into that loneliness and darkness comes God, as the dawning of a new day, and as a fresh breath to a dying lung.

The book culminates with the many ministries which can help us through our Slough of Despond. Help and Pliable came to assist Christian in *Pilgrim's Progress*. There are many ministries which lead us up, on and through. These come from many sources, but it is the God of each source that we find ourselves drawn nearer to through this book. There are many healings, but one and the self-same Spirit works through them all. Found as you are, you are left for the Spirit of God to work upon you.

Introduction[1]

T here was a noise in the distance. It was not a shout or a voice, it was as if someone was speaking whilst having a mouthful of food. It might have even been the shout of one who was muffled or gagged, or the sound of some distant, roaring football crowd when the goal has at last been scored. The voice came nearer, the sounds taking shape. At the same time lights began to shine in my head and then, as if dawn had suddenly dawned through the darkness, I was conscious. I could hear and see. The noises had been those of the hospital ward going about their daily work. I was on the four posts of sickness lying helplessly after a car accident. This wasn't Heaven. It wasn't hell. It wasn't in-between. "Where am I?" A nurse hurried to my side to comfort me and then it all came back, the accident, the impact, the screeching of brakes, the depth of impenetrable blackness as if a light had suddenly been turned out, black curtains drawn across a window. My eyes felt heavy again as if I was drifting, maybe even falling off the edge of the world and into the blackness of loneliness.

*　　*　　*

There are many theories about illness...why it happens, what the remedies are. Some ideas are not given to show us a way out or how to overcome sickness, indeed they seem to make us more conscious than ever that we have been caught in a snare. We need balance, we need to compare Scripture with Scripture, like with like, kind with kind, until the whole pattern found in the Bible comes together.

I do not write *In Sickness and in Health* from the aspect of the medical world. I have not written it as a bystander, nor as one of a crowd of onlookers. I do not bring thoughts before you simply from the mind and pen of other writers; I write them from a full heart and an overflowing soul which magnifies God my Saviour. What I have gleaned in passing through a number of major illnesses, I pass on to you.

There have been times, as in the Book of Ruth, when it has appeared as if "handfuls of purpose" have been left in my pathway (Ruth 2:16). I have not trodden these into the ground, but have lifted them up into my heart, thanking God for the Boaz who placed them there.

The hope is that those things which have helped me may help you and the comfort which has comforted me may comfort you also. May my strength give you strength, for does not the Scripture state: "Two are better than one"? (Ecclesiastes 4:9)

The great thing about help and comfort is that it is never ending. It reaches into all situations. It speaks with a thousand tongues into a thousand nations. It is a common language — the common language of the common people. Suffering is the lot of humanity. At some time in life you will pass through suffering. If you do not, then someone near and dear to you will be enduring a trial of their faith. It is at times like these that we can be of great help. That which has been put into us can be given to another until they, too, find themselves well and strong again. In the darkness of suffering, that which influences us can influence us for ever, for better or for worse.

When I had newly come to Christ my youngest brother went out one day never to return. He was 6 years of age and the next time I saw my brother he was in an undertaker's coffin. That could have driven me away over the hills and far away from God for ever, or it could have brought me closer to the God of all comfort and allowed me to discover the whole counsel of God regarding suffering for myself. I thank God that the latter was the case.

When it seems as if everything in life has given you up, then God is able to take you up and put something into you which will give you a deeper understanding of His nature. When we are Born Again the nature of Christ enters into us by His Holy Spirit (John 3:7). That nature has to be developed. It is like the solid block of gold from which the cherubim and the golden candlestick in the Old Testament were formed (Exodus 37:17). From one solid mass a shape, a new shape, which led to worship and held light for all to see was developed. How different from the words of Aaron when the golden calf was made: "I threw this in, and this came out" (Exodus 32:24). There was no beating in order to shape, no hammering for design. I am sure

that suffering can do the same for us all, worked on by Bezaleel —
meaning "the shadow of God" (Exodus 31:2; 36:1,2; 37:1). From that
process the gold takes glorious shape. From the green of youth the
gold of old age can be developed, even before we reach a certain
number of years or when our skin is worn and creased. It can come
to us at any time and it comes through the variations of life in which
we are all a part. Life, all of life, sunshine and shade, showers and
bowers, are meant to develop us into a maturity which trusts God in
all situations, a maturity which does not crumble or crack under the
slightest pressure. It is that which speaks of ripeness. The wind, rain,
storms, frost, sunshine have all fallen onto the developing fruit until
it reaches maturity — a maturity which is more than years, and more
than weight or height. It is more than family or country of origin, it
is that which is produced in a lovely walk before God. If we walk
with God then His shadow will fall across our path. We can act as
children do and run back into the sunshine. There is always the
choice of crossing to the sunny side of the street, but sometimes in
life there is no other side. We may even seek to jump across the shadows, just like the game we played when we were children — "Jump
the Shadow" — but one final thing we can do is to walk on in the
shadows until the sun breaks through again and the shadows of life
pass away, melted in the presence of the sun.

We must remind ourselves that to "afflict" means "to dash to the
ground"[2]. Jesus fell to the ground under the weight of the Cross
(Mark 15:21; Luke 23:26). A "trial" is that which exposes us fully,
that which is undergoing a process. "Tribulation" is taken from the
Roman meaning relative to a machine which separates chaff from
wheat. A "burden" is that which weighs heavily upon us, but instead
of the burden squeezing us into its mould we need to develop the
strength to lift it and use it to glorify God. Samson conquered with
the jawbone of an ass — "with the jawbone of an ass I have made an
ass of them" (Judges 15:16). It is a weight which can be turned into
a weight of glory!

There are things in life which will make a demand on one's
resources. It is then that we begin to recognise the resources which
are ours in Jesus Christ. We have to be brought into situations.
Many times those situations can loom as large as any Everest before

us, and it is at those times that we discover our resources. Even as fish, we swim near the surface, until the time of storm and then we go to the deep waters.

Whatever you are called to go through, remember you are "called" to go through! There are two alternatives through any difficulty with God or without God. There are times when the little brooch with the words "Jesus Saves" etched on it, or the metal Cross around your neck will not mean much, for it is the living Presence of the living Christ which we need to help us to grow in our circumstances. Then, instead of being under the circumstances, those same circumstances will be under us. Your choice is either to face it alone, or with God. I have made my choice, and that is to face the flinty things of life with the Lord Jesus Christ, Who set His face as a flint and said: "Courage; I have conquered" (John 16:33)[3]. I am going to conquer with Jesus the Conqueror, for He makes us more than conquerors! All conquerors are dead. We will live on forever in the power of an endless life. Our destiny is not death, nor is it life — it is durability with a God-given ability to conquer all things in His Name.

NOTES

1. The King James version of the Bible is used throughout, unless otherwise stated. The N.I.V. is the New International Version; R.S.V. the Revised Standard Version; A.S.V. the Authorised Standard Version.

2. "Afflict" from the Latin "fligo". See Chambers dictionary.

3. New English Bible translation.

1

Suffering and Sickness
defined and described

*All the king's horses and all the king's men
Couldn't put Humpty together again.*

It is the hurts, the pains, burdens and sores which make us part of humanity. Without them we would be just a floating leaf or feather passing by. We are all part of the Human Race, but some are in that Race as the walking wounded. We have goals we want to achieve, but because of suffering and sickness we are prevented from achieving. Some experience deep suffering, and in it they discover salt and wine.

When we define and describe suffering, when we feel we can talk about our sickness, we dethrone it, and its power becomes limited. It becomes a Limited Company. We need to recognise of all discomforts, they are only part of this life. Painful parts sometimes, but they are only for a time and season, until time shall be no more.

❋   ❋   ❋

We all have moments when questions without answers keep bouncing back into the hurt that has become a part of us. They possess an elasticity. There are times and hours of why? when? and whom? Just one-word questions that occur time after time. We demand answers concerning illness which "wastes at the noon-day" (Psalm 91:6). Somehow it seems that instead of the deep becoming more shallow and the darkness turning into light, the opposite becomes the truth. When we enter into such an experience, there is always a seeking of answers to our suffering.

Suffering can take the form of fear, feebleness, faintness, pain, shame, thorn, splinter, remorse, darkness and impending doom. Into life step all these things in the shape of worry and torment. It is as if a window has shattered, a bomb exploded, and the fragments have lacerated and as far as I'm concerned I was left scarred for life. One is left gazing at the ceiling or the blanket which covers the bed.

You might ask why a medical dictionary has never been written whereby, in alphabetical order, your sickness, your burdens, your fear and fret could be listed in order, so that you might easily thumb a page and turn up the answers.

If this were possible, such ditties as *Ring a ring of roses, a pocket full of posies, Atishoo! Atishoo! we all fall down!* would never have been written. These words were composed when the Black Death Plague killed so many people. They thought that every foul smelling disease was the breath of a demon and that the smell of the rose would ward off the deadly disease. Sweet smelling herbs or flowers were used to attempt to ward off sickness. At times like these we seek answers to questions which can never be answered. The answers seem to be as monarchs in ivory palaces, untouched and unmoved by questioning or reasoning. I am always left trying to unravel the unattainable. The tears I have shed have had no softening power. They cannot be moulded as clay in the hands of the potter. The problem of pain and the painful questions are plentiful indeed.

The questioning of our suffering

There are some questions which have to be asked and there are some questions which should never be asked, for there are no ready made answers. There is no tablet, drug, medicine bottle or consultant's pen which contains the answer to every ailment, yet we all desire answers which will turn malady into music and suffering into song. There is no panacea for polarised pain.

Why do we suffer? Why is one healed and not another? Why are some kept from suffering at all, while others are not? Why do some die and sink as ships which have hardly left harbour, so young, so vulnerable, so lovely? One question answered creates another that will never be answered.

Although the pain of suffering is still dark and foreboding, there are many answers provided in New Testament Scriptures which are there for our learning. They are not meant to be there just to echo into our situation and mock us with their emptiness. There are some arguments and answers given which are as much use as steam coming from a boiling kettle, and there are still the conundrums which can never be answered by what the minds of men can conjure up. Jesus came, not to give all the answers to pain and suffering but to fill that hurt, that weakness, that burden with His Presence. He came that we might understand suffering through His living, His being and His teaching.

There is an old Irish proverb which says, *Every invalid is a physician*. This is how the words, "Physician, heal thyself", can be fully implemented.

The different patterns of suffering

There are chinks of light in texts such as in Romans 8:18, 28:

> *"For I reckon the sufferings of this present time are not worthy to be compared with the glory which shall be revealed in us...All things work together for good to them that love God, who are called according to His purposes."*

Philippians 3:10 — *"The fellowship of His sufferings." "For a little while you may have to suffer grief in all kinds of trials..."* 1 Peter 1:6 N.I.V. These have come so that your faith — of greater worth than gold which perishes even though refined by fire may be proved genuine. Even when we have quoted the text it can seem but chaff without corn. There is just the empty shell. We need such a fulness that will spill over into our lives and flood them with hope so great and assurance so mighty that it cannot be measured. When that happens evidences of our suffering are not worth counting. There is such a need for great assurance. We need to know that God knows. We must know that there is a pattern being formed in life. Something I can learn, know and see for myself. This eases pain.

While in a measure we have portions of Scripture which enlighten us, we can still be left with more questions unanswered than answers given. It is cold comfort to quote a text over a telephone. The icicles have formed before the hearer has heard! When a corpse is lying in the same room then the mourner needs a sense of direction and the Presence of Him Who said, "Blessed are those who mourn for they shall be comforted" (Matthew 5:4).

The wounds which can cause deep suffering

A sudden telephone call to tell that a loved one has been suddenly snatched from you: you have just been informed that your child has suspected meningitis: your teenage son has become a drug addict and is stealing cars to finance his habit, or leaving home to live in a flat with his friends...you pass him in the street or glimpse him through the car window looking drawn, ill and tired. What can you do with such a sickness? It is as a heavy sack on your back. When the emotions dry up, when there is no bandage large enough to cover the wound, the hurt and the depth of anguish can be alleviated just a little by friends, by compassion, by love — it is a help that comes from outside ourselves. There is a need for broader, deeper understanding. We need to be where compassion reigns. There are people who are not only walking wounded, but are sleeping, waking and grieving wounded. There are areas of healing in the Word of God. There are ministries required to the body, soul and spirit. Sometimes the illness can be of the mind and not of the body. Sickness is more than physical, it can be spiritual, it can be mental, something you cannot see or stitch, parts that other medicines cannot reach. When that happens we need a touch from the Hand which holds the worlds. There is a God Who cares enough to cry over corruption of sickness, a God Who died to help us with it, in it and through it. There is a God Who cares for the careworn, the wounded, a God Who loves the lifeless. Jesus said: "I am among you as one Who serves" (Luke 22:27). There is enough in Christ to scatter care to the very core of the calamity! He is here to help the helpless and to give hope to the hopeless. There has to be that in us which learns to lean and is bent to the leaning position through the burdens placed upon us. Trust God in the park and in the dark!

The unreachable pains of suffering

There are times when we are reaching out but touch nothing. There are moments in illness when one goes to bed, hoping that this may be the last night and there will be no awakening. Even when attending a funeral there can be a feeling of being more dead than the corpse in the coffin. They are nailed in and surrounded by a wooden prison. Jesus came to heal the broken-hearted and to set free those who are held captive. It may not happen all at once, but it will happen! It does not always come along the channels we may expect it to. A light suddenly surprises a Christian, shining when it isn't time for the dawn. No-one switched it on, it is an inner light, a Godly glow. We get to know certain things, precious, deep and lasting lustres through ways into which we are led. From the position of pain there is many a gain. Not every lesson can be learned from a text book or blackboard and chalk. Not every element of education comes from the classroom, college or university. The School of Life and the department called "Suffering" is out there in the world at large. Some lessons received and understood do not place letters after the name, but they do form the letters of the character and make us into the right type of person. Pain bridges the great gulf which is fixed between us and God.

The helps of God in suffering

God does not walk in men's shoes. He does not come and knock at the door. He sometimes comes in through the window. He slides in on a laugh or He marches in clothed in a thought. He is the painter of pain, and He works through a word from Scripture, through a friend or through a hospital. God can and does work through faith. Many medicines march with Him. Faith and pain are in partnership with Him. A nurse, a doctor, a Minister, a friend, a Bible verse...all these things work together for good to them that love God. We can pass through a difficulty arm in arm and hand in hand with God, or we can pass through it alone without Him, but whichever way, we still must go through to the other side.

God is building character and fortitude. Sometimes we do not like or recognise the tools He uses for building. There is a patience to be discerned through pain. In that which is broken, that which is whole can be found. In the New Testament the alabaster box of perfume or ointment was just cold slate, cold crust until it was broken (Mark 14:3). Then it revealed a perfume, imprisoned in the shell, the contents of which filled the house and cooled the Saviour's feet.

The darkness mental suffering can bring

When people pass through mental illness there is a great gulf — an outer blackness. It seems as if Heaven is brass and the earth we walk on is just a pile of stones. Every step seems as if we are walking through fire. That which we have known, suddenly becomes less known. The things of which we were so sure, become less sure, almost as if some cataract is growing over the eye and clouding the vision. We are robbed of our rigid confidence and become clothed in cold incredulity. Disorder can rob us of our assurances and our sensibilities. So many people are still ignorant of certain types of illnesses. There is a total lack of understanding. If you are not running, jumping, playing and working then you are considered to be an oddity of the first degree. Suddenly that which I was so confident of becomes a Will-o-the-Wisp. Confidence is fragmented, the mind is tormented. Drugs appear to remove everything into a far off land and added to the problem is the perplexity of thinking that the body will never heal, the mind will never be right again. It will be as right as rain when it is raining! That which is upon you is more than rain, it is a storm in full flood! You are told to "Pull yourself together!" Yet you cannot, because the parts have drifted so far apart. You are told "It will be alright on the night!" Yet you are in the night, and it is not alright. When we see as God sees, we look on things as God looks on them and we understand as God understands. God does not just look on or look in from the outside, He is on the inside, looking out.

The trust which triumphs in suffering

Corrie Ten Boom said, "When you are travelling on a train and that train goes through a dark tunnel, you don't throw away your ticket, you just sit back and trust the engineer".[1]

To those who enter into the hospital of hurt and the out-patient room of pain without real pity, life can be tragic and traumatic. It is almost as if someone has drawn the curtains on your life. What is needed is that which will open those curtains again and let the sun shine in. This book has been written to help the healing process. If I can lighten your burden or your darkness, then we shall have glorious success.

Where once prayer was a delight and preaching, witnessing and fellowshipping were all the order of the day, quite suddenly the thorns appear. What is this gloom, this terror, this blackness into which the hand of fate has thrust me? My expectations have not only been cut off, they have been made to be as if they were never there. The root, the branch, the flower, the leaf and the fruit have all withered. I am not like the man in Psalm 1 who has been transplanted and is by the river of water, whose leaf does not wither (Psalm 1:3). It is at this point that we are beginning to enter into the misery of suffering, to provide a ministry of suffering and to make us one with others.

Learning vital lessons from the suffering of others

Men come into our sick room — men like Daniel, Hezekiah, David, Trophimus, Epaphroditus, Paul and Job, ah yes, Job. I begin to identify with him and with all that which surrounded him. The pain, however deep, did not drown him. Those from north, south, east or west are not greater than Job. I learn with Job to sing in the minor key — "I know that my Redeemer lives". "Though He slay me, yet shall I praise Him". "Though worms destroy this body of flesh, I shall see Him for myself, and not another" (Job 13:15; 19:25-27). This is what I want to hear! This is what I want to be! It has taken real sickness to bring them to me and to stand or sit me amongst them! I knew mentally about their suffering and their faith, but now I am allowed to enter into it and to rub shoulders with them. It turned Job into an Apostle of affliction and endurance. He came forth from it all as a block of gold during the time of recession! I can listen to men like this, who have their fingers stained with ointments and their spoons still wet with the medicine. They bear in their spirits and their bodies the marks, the medals of suffering. In life all I have worn so far has been a medallion. It needs to be turned into a medal. It is at times like this that we have to simply wait before God and rediscover Him, see Him through the eyes of pain and hear Him with ears which are surrounded by suffering sounds. Wounds and hurt have a language all of their own. I must learn the language of suffering. I must live its life. To know God in pain is to know God with such a depth. When I am in a storm and the winds are raging, the waves are boisterous, seeming to touch the sky, then I have to say with Peter: "Lord, if it be Thou, bid me come to Thee on the water" (Matthew 14:28). Then, and only then, will my faith walk on water to Jesus Christ. We walk in another realm, in another dimension. There are parts of Noah's Ark which deep waters are going to test. When I visit an art gallery I don't have to paint pictures to compete with the work which has already been accomplished, I go to gaze and to learn by gazing. The same applies if I visit some large modern housing estate. I am not there to lay bricks, I look at the finished work of architect, builder, plumber, electrician. In my illness I have to learn to just let go and let God. That means letting God do what He desires to do. It means being able to see from the tangled mesh a tapestry coming forth which is woven by the Hand of God, a variety performance of colour, shape, shade and size. Sickness spices life. Up to now in my sickness I have been gazing on the back side of the tapestry and it has made no sense to me. When I step over to God's side then it makes sense and the pattern becomes visible. I see it from where God is and that sheds glorious light into all my darkened corners. I don't know who switched the light off, but I do know that someone has switched it on again! "I know in Whom I have believed, and that He is able to keep that which I have committed unto Him against that day" (2 Timothy 1:12). In the past, I believed, but now I know not only WHY I believe, but WHOM I believe. He has been able to reach and understand what I could never have reached or understood. Ruin becomes Resurrection! That which was dark is suddenly light in the Lord. I have to be taught to simply relax in His Presence. When and where a life of activity comes to a cliff edge, then I must stop and simply trust Him.

Suffering can be conquered through trusting

In sickness I do not feel like trusting God. There is confusion within and without. My depression is so deep that a human voice cannot reach me. I feel that the tide is rising and the boat is not rising with it. The sea is so vast and my boat so small. The sea is shoreless and shallowless — my boat fills with water. There is jeopardy all around. There is danger and peril. Sometimes the illness is so severe that I do not know if I do trust God. The doubts which lurked in the shadows and around the corners when I was in full health suddenly appear, amassed as if some trumpet had been blown and had called them to war against me. They rise up and declare: "We will not have this man to rule over us!" (Luke 23:18). When I count the doubts and then realise how few doctors, nurses, family and friends there are, the doubts seem so many. I seem to be so small. I am all at sea in a drifting, open boat. I seek a Columbus or a Captain Cook or Francis Drake to deal with this Armada! The pain is so real and I have no pill to pacify its cry and longing for release. I am left only with God. I have an emptiness. I am at the bottom of myself.

Suffering helps us to understand the important things in life

When illness comes to a life and a family it is the knock of the wolf at the door, and it is then that we really begin to examine and re-examine all that we have been taught. The things which we thought mattered the most suddenly matter the least. In the light of Eternity the true perspective of life is seen, heard and found. It is through ill-ness, many times, that we are brought into a place of belief. We previously have some mental acceptance, but because of illness, the colours are deepened into the fabric. At the end I know not only what I believe, but I have discovered that what was previously blind belief has now become reasoned faith and Hebrews 11:1 reminds me that it is a substance, it is an evidence, a title deed of things hoped for. It is the mental, physical and emotional pressures of life which bring out the best and the worst in us all.

The ravages of sin are still with us. We readily gave answers to others who suffered, quoting that which had never happened to us. If you cannot swim it is no use standing on a river bank instructing someone who is drowning! The answers for ourselves must come through God. There are things we can read in books, which are never ours because of our lack of experience of them. The things which happen to us during life, those things are ours. God uses time to tick the replies which are placed into our souls until we know that all things work together (Romans 8:28), all things symphonise, from the big bass drum to the triangle, not just as the instruments in an orchestra or the notes in a favourite tune, but they work for good to make an harmonious sound.

Suffering makes friends of enemies and strangers

All those discordant happenings, that illness, that breakdown, that which seems to cut me off and place me on one side and apart from the rest, work together for good. There is a blending in the mending. There is help in the forthcoming health. The darkest hour comes before the dawn. The disappointments become appointments with which to defeat opponents.

There is a word which we need, a help which is sought, and an open ear to listen to us which can do more than the physical physician whom we consult. There has to be that understanding of a higher realm in our heart. There is a greater power at work. There are diversity of diseases, yet there is manifold, many coloured grace (1 Peter 1:6; 4:10) folded one fold after another, but the folds have to be straightened in order to receive that grace with all its diverse aspects which, through the mantle of mourning, I have to discover. It is only after the event that I discover what I have uncovered as I have passed through my Valley of the Shadow of Death. Only then have I discovered that I, tremulous I, feared no evil (Psalm 23:4). I only realised this when I had passed through that darkness. Looking back I can see the light, but at the time, as I looked forward, there was no light. It is in the Valley, with all its shadows and monster-like boulders, in the parts where the sun does not shine and where the wind howls, it is there that I was discovered and it is there I make the discoveries of new worlds and unheard of planets, it is there I learn all about God and my own nature. Sickness and what I learn through it, always runs in two directions — that which I learn about God, and that which God learns about me. Is my faith as strong or as wrong as I thought? The hard parts He softens and, once softened, He indelibly stamps.

In all sickness, as Shakespeare says, "The misery of it does aquaint us with strange bedfellows". There is no stranger bedfellow than the sickness itself! Through it all, in it all and beyond it all I have discovered every one of these strange bedfellows for myself. To understand another, as the old Indian saying has it: "You must walk in their moccasins for at least three days before you make a serious or a series of judgements of another".

The deeper teachings of suffering and pain

Even nursery rhymes had their weaknesses! Jack falls down a hill, and the old remedy is to wrap his head in vinegar and brown paper. All we have sometimes is vinegar and brown paper! It is so basic. If that is all I receive from illness, then I am poor, wretched and blind indeed. The vinegar, the brown paper — not pink or white, not wine, but vinegar. Wasn't there a better substance, a more enduring substance that Jack's head might have been wrapped in? Didn't someone think of a bandage, or a plaster? Was there no one to heal or help? With all the modern help, with all the equipment which science has discovered there is still a deeper need of wanting to know if God is in this with me. Does God understand my situation? Is this carved on His Hands? Like Job, I must learn to receive good and evil from the Hand of the Lord (Job 2:10). What I am passing through or have passed through, has it passed through the Eternal's knowledge and way of understanding things? Has God seen it all with His all-seeing eye? Has it slid gently from His Hand? Has God allowed me to be slapped like a child? Was there something He has missed? Was I in that something that was missed? Questions... questions...until my soul and tongue become a questionnaire! They build up until I find I am facing a mountain which I am too weak to climb. The ladder of my thinking is smaller than the wall which I have to climb. The well is deep and dark and I have nothing with which to draw from it. I have to discover Jesus sitting on the side of the well. The darkness is so deep that light will not penetrate. Somewhere along the way the torch has been blown from my hand by a fierce wind and I have to search in order to produce new light. The word of the surgeon, the doctor, the physician, the minister — call them what you will, their words have seemed like rubber balls bouncing on concrete. They will not sink it. They float like flotsam and jetsam in my sea of hurt and injury. I must know if God is with me in all this. I want the evidence of God's Presence the most when I am ill, yet I feel that He is so absent in my mourning and my difficulties. I want to meet with the God of pain, love, joy, peace, healing. That God must not be cast in bronze, slate or cold marble. He must not be made like the Roman gods. He must be made like His brethren. Whatever the Romans did not fully understand, they made a god of, and it would crumble and topple as age gave it a gentle nudge. God is not a God of things but a God of all things, including sickness and health. I have to meet with all things in God. I have to make Him Lord of every situation. I have to see Him as the Creator and Sustainer of all things. We must pass through the alphabet of life. We cannot live in the "A" for ever, we must go from A to Z. It is then that I begin to make fresh discoveries. The God who only rode on laughter as on a white steed, or sat upon the joke, the smile, the pleasure, now appears in the sickness as He appeared on the Emmaus Road. The bubble of emotion has burst. The God of the mind only is not there, for the mind is full of other things. The God who was only a ditty or a chorus, or even a hymn, is not there — the "Lord of all being throned afar"[2] — like a star is so cold and remote, for I am unable to sing, shine or shout. I cannot express myself as freely as the wind. The storm which has enveloped me has torn up the trees and laid flat the houses. It has swollen the rivers to an overflowing devastation. I must find God in a new and deeper dimension. I must go down to the depths to find the God of the heights. I have known God as pleasure and treasure, but now, O, but now, I have entered into a new discovery. There is a new trail which I must follow which will help me to help others, which will enable me to comfort with the comfort that I am comforted with, to strengthen with my new strength of spirit. I want to live a full life, but God must fill that life. There were parts and corners where God was left out. What measures He has had to take to bring every part of my life into oneness with Him!

Suffering can be baptized in discovery

I must discover that God is more than intellect, more than service, more than shine and shout. God is something and Someone deeper than anything this life can express. I discover this depth, this mind of wealth, this bottle of health through that which He has allowed to come upon me. As I reach, through faith, and touch the nettle, it turns into a primrose.

God has shown me in the fulness of His nature of light, in the strong beam of things, that I can live without all the things I thought were necessary in my life. Those things which can be removed are removed, and those things which remain are the Eternal things of God. It is God and God alone that I must come into contact with. I have found, whilst I was healthy, wealthy and strong, that the garments they wrapped God in were so thick that I could not touch Him. When I reached out I only touched that which surrounded Him. When I worshipped and prayed it was to a far off figure, cemented and seated in theology and books, surrounded by all manner of attendants. God has had to strip away all these, so that if I were cast on some desert island, and illness can be just that, then I will be satisfied with Him. I will be one with Him in the years which are past, in the present, and just as contented in future years. The discovery has been made...If God is for us, who can be against us (Romans 8:31)? He is more than all that which is against us: *"That which is formed against you shall not prosper"*.

I have found that God is not subject to change, as my body is subject to change. God is not as that which can be tasted, handled or dissipated. He grows not weary. He neither slumbers nor sleeps (Psalm 121:4). He cares for me, and He says, "Cast all your care on Me, for it matters to Me about you" (1 Peter 5:7; Knox's translation). I have not learned that truth as some equation or mathematics table. I have not learned it as I would the ABC. It is not a television truth, nor is it of calculator content. It is through disease, being unconscious, drifting between death and life — these things have been stamped on my spirit — not written on water as before, but written with a pen of iron on my rock nature. Written by the pen of experience, held in the Hand of God. Written in the light of His Word, revealing, healing.

NOTES

1. Source unknown.

2. *Redemption Hymnal,* hymn no. 1, O.W.Holmes (Assemblies of God, 114/6 Talbot Street, Nottingham NG1 5GH).

Patience: The Royal Law of Suffering

It is sickness and suffering which makes us part of the same parcel as Job. In this patriarch our pains are seen as shadows, and they are eased. We lay on the same couch, and sit in the same chair. His healing becomes my healing. They are eased, and I am helped when I realise that the man with great patience and prosperity did not suffer for his own sin or wrong doing. Job did not suffer for his own mistakes, and God wasn't trying to crush him to humble him. Because he loved God he was afflicted. As a righteous man he was challenged. The character of all who believe will be tested because they do and will believe. There is the unfolding of the nature of faith. That faith is revealed as more precious than things, than gold which perishes. There are depths discovered in this sufferer which are as deep as the mine from where gold comes from. Like Abraham and you, he staggered not, but remained faithful whatever was brought into his life. That patience of God was discovered and uncovered in him. There are discoveries to be made in all of us. There are hidden qualities which only the fires of temptation and suffering will reveal. He became an object lesson for all the Ages. Those who find themselves in deep waters, can reach out, and take something from Job which will lead them to safety.

❊ ❊ ❊

Job has become synonymous with suffering, patience and pain. His "comforters" gather around every sick bed and they bear every coffin (Job 2:11)! They become as crumbs between the sheets!

Job was a real person, not just a poetical figure — Ezekiel Chapter 14:14 and 20 prove this. The Book of Job is more than literature or poetry, it is a science, an explanation of suffering. It is the technical teaching of truth about trial. Job became the vehicle of

God for victory, as did David when facing Goliath. God used David, even as He used Job to defeat Satan and all the old theories of sickness and trial.

The Book and the life of Job are a "theodicy" — a Greek word meaning "to justify God". These words express fully those written at the foot of Milton's statue: "To assert Eternal Providence and to justify the ways of God to men."

The prosperous person suffers

Job was a Gentile whom God had prospered, and that in itself is an amazing thing, that God should so bless and try one of the Gentile nature, and include also his Gentile friends. We have a ready-made play acted before our very eyes. Not a play in a theatre, but one that is acted out in every home in the land at some time. The theatre becomes the heart. Shakespeare said the world was a stage and we are but the actors, the performers. Sometimes that stage can be a wheelchair, a bed of sickness, a hospital ward, a frustrating room in one's own home. The scene is set with problematic burdens or some anxiety which seems to stretch the mind beyond its normal elasticity. Through and in Job we are taken backstage, to see the workings, rather like the Granada Studio Tours in Manchester where one is taken backstage, to see how all the television programmes are made. It is as if the clock maker has opened the back of a grandfather clock and is explaining all the spinning wheels and the springs. As humans we can only gaze on the face of things, it is God Who sees the inner workings.

The children of God suffer

Job is a man. He is God's man, yet sickness and suffering and his reactions make him our man also. Job needs to come and be with us, dwell with us in our sickness and in our darkest moments. The Bible teaches that he does, in the Person of Jesus Christ.

The blanket of sickness and darkness which covers him stretches throughout the ages to each one of us. Sickness speaks every language and walks every street. It visits every home. It is found in commerce and it is found in palaces. We can tear that blanket into pieces and make those pieces into swathing bands to bind up our own putrefying wounds. It is then that we find there is a balm in God. The doctrines found in the Book of Job can be as a medicine. Understanding comes into finite minds of the Infinite Mind. When we face illness we stand as children looking over a sea of salty waters. We cannot understand it. It is so large, so deep, so wide. We need the Christ Who walks on water; the Christ Who sails the boat; the Christ Who commands the storm to be stilled; the Christ Who takes fish even from these waters (Mark 4:39). Sickness, worry, sighing and sadness are enlightened through Job.

We have a point at which to commence in our suffering. There are New Testament lights and sidelights which, when switched on in a darkened sickroom can flood that room with a brilliance beyond the midday sun. From every part of that room can come the quiet voice of assurance which we find in the Word of God, bringing a certainty that One has been here and has gone this way before, to smooth out the path and to lessen the pain at its deepest point. Whatever depth you sink, you will find Jesus Christ at the top and at the bottom. He stands on the shore of everything. Christ is there, wearing a Crown of Thorns on His head (John 19:2).

The chosen and the choice suffer

If you were to take away all that we have revealed to us about suffering through Job, what would we have? We would be like a child lost in the shadows in the corner of a room, the light switch too high for that child to reach to enable him to switch the light on. We would be left to measure our illness by the dark shadow of the room. It would be like many publications on evolution. In the space of a few pages we read, "It might have been"... "It could have been"... "It should have been"... "It might have been so"... "We suggest it was"... "Perhaps it was so"... guesses — question marks for ever!

Job and the Book of Job alters all that. In the Old Testament the concept of sickness was that if you suffered, then you had sinned. If you suffered, then you were proud and not righteous. A good man just did not suffer! The Book of Job was written to refute those arguments. We can be pure, holy, happy, harmless and undefiled and yet sickness can come as a cloud, blotting out the sun. It is at that time that we need the Son of Righteousness, with healing in His wings (Malachi 4:2)!

Sickness declares that God does not care. It is the voice of atheism. There is probably more atheism in sickness than in any other thing. The doctrines of unbelief can be sown during a prolonged illness. They are there to attack man's soul. They are there to wither our healthy trust and faith. Sickness is to blind the eye and twist the foot. It is there to give us a wrong image of God. It was so even before Job or Jesus. The Book of Job itself needs the light of the New Testament to complete the revelation of God in sickness. Without that revelation we, in our understanding, can be like children daubing paint everywhere thinking it is a masterpiece!

There are no ceremonies, no laws of Moses, no battles of Joshua, Fall of man or many repeated laws of Leviticus — all of these are missing and without them, as in the Day of Grace, man is justified before his Maker.

The righteous person suffers

Old ideas about sickness, sin, pride and rebellion, suffering in sickness for our sin, all these are smashed to dust with a great hammer. They are dead and buried, cast into a bottomless pit. Job proves a man can be righteous. He proves his integrity can be intact. He proves he can be serving God, a good man, blameless, eschewing evil, and yet the stroke of sickness can fall upon him, not to break him but to bend him and to find him worshipping God. Sickness need not be the whip which drives us away from God. It can be the gentle hand which brings us closer to Him. It can be that which deepens and enriches our experience in God, almost like dropping stones into water until it overflows. When God gathers the stones, it is then that the water has been turned into wine.

The members of every family suffer

Job lived in the land of Uz (Job 1:1). He was a family man with great convictions about God, so much so that he daily offered prayers and sacrifices for his family lest they sinned (Job 1:5). We are introduced to him in his prosperous state. Change what he has, and see what happens — that was Satan's argument. Touch his flesh and in doing so stagger his faith. Remove his riches and make bare the poverty of his soul. Take from him and he will withdraw from God. The principle of an eye for an eye will be revealed. Whatever the strength of his devotion to God, it will weaken under sickness. If God touches his skin, his flesh and bone, then faith will falter as it staggers (Job 2:5). It did not happen! Satan had spread yet another lie! Sickness can prove Satan wrong. Love has to learn to lean. It has to learn to interpret "other tongues". God allowed Satan to attack Job. He allowed Job to be led into temptation in order to bring out the best in him. Sickness was allowed and was used to discover Job. There are latent propensities which only ill health can discover. When discovered by God, the weakness is made strong by faith. God always tries us, to bring out the best in us, like placing metal into the fire to see it purified. Satan works through the opposite principle. He wants to see the metal disintegrate. He wants to see the worst in us brought to the fore. Satan desires to see the contents of the fire of suffering turned into ashes, to become an insult, a slap in the face of the Almighty God. It is the time of the sowing of the tares in the field at night.

All believers suffer

Adam Clarke,[1] commenting on Genesis 22:1, says "God did 'tempt' Abraham". The word "tempt" means "try". It suggests the unfurling of colour, the unfolding of a flag as it flutters in the breeze. It means to pierce, as if light has come through a hole or a crack. It describes Israel's banners. As they marched, any shining object or broken piece of pottery which would glisten in the sun was attached to their banners. The sun caught the object and flashed it into the world around. This put fear into the enemies of Israel, because they thought they were going to face an army of light.

In the New Testament, among the Greeks, if you went to purchase a vessel and wanted to test it, then you walked out of the shadows of the bazaar into the open sunlight. The vessel was held up and if it had a crack or had been filled with wax, the sunlight discovered it. They tested the vessel with sunlight for two reasons — to see whether it was the genuine article, and to check that it was sincere, i.e. free from wax (Ephesians 6:24; Titus 2:7).

At the conclusion of the story of Abraham offering Isaac as a sacrifice to God, it was Isaac who was under the knife, not Abraham (Genesis 22:2). The young man would have been a good age at the time of this offering on Mount Moriah. Some think he could have been as old as thirty, and would have been well able to overcome the old man, Abraham. He didn't. He submitted himself to the point of the knife. Abraham was about to plunge it into the breast of his promised heir when he noticed a ram caught in the thicket. Again, the picture of suffering is presented to us in the thicket. It was the thicket which provided the offering and sacrifice. The very thing our trials do for us is seen in these happenings. Every sorrow should point us to the Man of Sorrows (Isaiah 53:3).

The Book of Job is an exposition of how we act under discipline, of how we react under the knife and in the thicket. Do we groan and moan, kick and struggle? Do we learn that it is hard for us to kick against the pricks (Acts 9:5; 26:14)? Do we learn the sharp lessons of the knife point? In it all, Abraham heard the voice of God, loud and clear, calling to him.

The peaceful person suffers

Job had peace with God. He had a great relationship with Him. There was no man in the East quite like Job (Job 2:3). Young and old rose in his presence, and even placed their hands over their mouths. Suddenly, there is an eruption and what was so smooth and peaceful becomes frantic, prancing. Job sees God in anger, plaguing him, seeking to destroy him, tormenting him, hunting, seeking, chasing, charging at him. Job 6:4, he saw himself as the target and the Almighty sending arrows of pain and destruction into him. It is the feeling of the spinning clay on the potter's wheel, the clay in the kiln unable to see the potter's face, hear his voice or understand his intentions. Dresden china has to be fired twice, once in the fire is not enough. It has to be returned for a second scorching, burning, heating. Life among the flames is so hot, yet it is twice placed there until its lustre far outshines that of others. That loved, glazed piece, with pattern so gilded, appears to commend the work of the artist to the world. Diamonds are polished in their own dust.

The complete person suffers

The whole story is revealed in the Book of Job. God and Satan along with Job's friends, and Elihud who comes in at the end, is placed there for good measure (Job 32: 2, 4, 5, 6). Everything that happened to Job has to be examined by the New Testament. There are many things unanswered through the suffering of Job which are only answered in the New Testament. In Job we only have part of the puzzle. It all comes together in the New Testament, even as all the promises of God are fulfilled in the Book of Revelation. The Old and the New Testament is the difference between a medical student looking at a case of illness, and a mature consultant.

According to the Book of Job, he charged not God foolishly (Job 1:22). He put his hand over his mouth, even as God placed His hand over the life of Job, to act as a cover.

There are some who fall at the first hurdle. The first touch of pain or sight of blood, and they are into a faint which becomes an escape hatch. They fall and falter when the test is applied to them. There are others who sink when sickness pays them a visit, knocking on the door with a bony skeletal hand. How will Job fare? Is there something hidden, something lurking in the shadows which will spring forth, revealed by the severe trials? Will he buckle or crack?

Those who love God suffer

Remove from him his prosperity, his fine garments of linen trimmed with gold, adorned with rich jewels, and his service and usefulness to God will be withdrawn (Job 2:5). Royalty and finery will become rags. There will be no advantage for him to continue to glorify God as his Maker. Will he fall away when earthly advantage is removed? When the darkness comes creeping over vale and hill will his candle be blown out, or will it flare into a great fire, so great that sacrifice can be offered upon it? The sacrifices of the yielding heart, trusting, responding, knowing that God will do the right thing. When all the props of family, friends and wealth are lost, when the admiration and hand clapping of men has gone, what will he be like then? Such is the cynical reasoning of men. Men whom sickness has not mellowed or softened, but hardened instead. They must be proved wrong by a lump of clay. Through part of God's creation a human being, Satan and all his hordes must be put to shame. All the fears, feelings, emotions of Job must be brought into subjection to faith and God's measure of things. Job proves that God's thorns, hurt and pain are better than Satan's flowers. One of God's hurts are worth more than a flower shop owned by the enemy! God's weeds are more to be gathered and garlanded than all the flowers of Satan. Job is unaware of the things that are taking place behind the curtain of Eternity and suffering. He comes to realise that even if the rod is raised, then the closer you get to the One Who is wielding it, the gentler the blows are. There is no room for force, it has been removed in the position of closeness.

God is re-writing what pain and suffering are all about. He is giving it a new look, a new history of sickness and the part it plays in life is being written and God is the historian. It is written by the finger of God, that same finger which wrote the decalogue in stone and rock. That finger is now writing an explanation. In all this, the enemy of man, the enemy of Job, your enemy, the enemy of Jesus, is being withheld (Job 2:6). There is a greater power. Sickness wrapped in suffering is only allowed when and where and how much by God alone. Using suffering, God is painting the glory of it through the life of Job, a life which testifies to all and helps all, because part of your load is part of Job's load, and all that load is placed on Jesus. Job suffered knowing so little. We suffer knowing so much! We have a wooden Cross on a hill as the backdrop to our sufferings. We know of a Death, a suffering, a Resurrection and a Second Appearing of Jesus Christ.

The mature person suffers

Job 1:1 says, Job was "perfect". However, this does not mean that he was complete in every part. He was complete in a measure. An instrumentalist assumes he can play a musical instrument, until he hears a master play! I can play the piano, but when I listen to Mozart, I can't play at all!

Job was as entire as a ship with full complement, ready to sail. The problem was, he had never sailed. He had never faced the uncertain waters with their ferocity or depth. He was complete, perfect as some new instrument, but he had never been played. There are parts of life which have to be tested to the full. You will see on some cranes the words "breaking point", suggesting maximum weight. It is the weight they have been tested to, the strength of the steel rope written on it. It is easy to be a dead Apostle, mentioned in the Bible...it is easy to be a cardboard Christian. The model in the shop window is perfect, but it is cold. It is perfection without heart. To be in a book or framed in a picture is so easy, yet it is unreal. It is not life or living. It has to be taken out of that which removes it from the world. Find out if it works. How does it react in situations of adversity? We can all roll downhill, but what about the uphill struggle? We live in a real world of terrorism, the bomb, the bullet, hatred, strife, decision making and challenge. One boat is as good as another in dry dock! The soldier in the barracks has never been tested until he enters the field of human conflict. Job, as with us, had to be tested before he could be rested. He had to undergo scrutiny in every department of his life. Have no fear, if he is the genuine article, ready to receive God's mark of approval, it will only be received after trial. As with our British "kite mark", it is only placed on goods that we can have confidence in, goods which have been tried and tested and not found wanting. The suffering will not detract from but will add to. Pained in every part, but not torn apart. Being made to fit perfectly into the palm of God's plan!

The ordinary person suffers

When God wants to colour a character, when He wants to blend colour with colour and kind with kind, when He wants to arrange it so that it does not wash off during the slightest shower, He blends it deep. God wants that which will not brush off as people come alongside us. Powder paint is no good! God uses sick beds! What is so bland, so base, has to take on new pigment and shape, different shades, mixing colour with colour in order to produce a third colour. This is what God is doing. To the ordinary eye it is unseen, as with Job. We need to pray the prayer of Elisha for the young man who couldn't see anything but mountains when he was in the valley..." Lord, open the eyes of the young man" (2 Kings 6:17). He saw the valley filled with horses and horsemen.

Life is not a bunch of rags tied together at both ends by a birth and a death. It is something more glorious and has a greater design than that. "The King's daughter is all glorious within...her clothing is of wrought gold...all her garments smell of aloes, cassia and the attire of all perfumes" (Psalm 45:13). Job proves this beyond all reasonable doubt when, at the end, he comes forth as gold...not rust or metal (Job 23:10). He has been purified from the dross. Job, in the strictest sense is an Apostle of Suffering. He was a pioneer, establishing the righteousness of God through suffering. He was stepping into the darkness of the darkest night to find God was in that darkness. He understood things that were difficult to understand. He came out from them better than he went into them, like a deep sea diver coming to the surface with a handful of pearls. Like the Psalmist, Job could say, "Before I was afflicted, I went astray" (Psalm 119:67).

There is no weary sufferer who is not highly indebted to the patriarch of Uz. He too has left footsteps for us to follow. There are more sure places to walk, and we can breathe a sigh of unutterable relief because of this man Job. I, by faith, with all these men of affliction, must accept the ways of God, sometimes leading through dark caverns, in shade and in sunshine. These ways are winding ways at times.

Suffering and trial came to Job in four different ways. This gives us the complete square of suffering. It is not disjointed. It is not fragmented. We do not peer at it through some dark glass. We behold it face to face. It is given to us as a whole, so that we, looking at it, can learn, and the Lord can give us understanding in all things as we meditate upon them.

(a) Suffering came through family loss

Job 1:2. Seven sons and three daughters. The perfect number in a family gathering. Job 1:5... Job wonders if they might curse God in their hearts. I think he means whether they might forget God? He sanctified them, he made offerings for them. He was one with his family and his influence was felt right through his ancestry. They were a close knit community. Troubles and trials do spring from within. Job 1:5, Thus did Job continually...everything was going on in the same way — day followed day, night followed night...everything was taking its natural course, when suddenly the blade went into the soil and that soil was the soul of Job! Calamity struck. The Sabeans came and carried them away (Job 1:15)! Along with this great weight came news of another catastrophe — Chapter 1:18...the wind from the wilderness came and pushed the house down. Shakespeare's words are so true: *"Come not single foes, but in battalions"*. Misfortunes never come singly, they come with large armies. Yet still Job retains his spirituality, for he recognises that they came from Heaven. Fire and wind from Heaven. Every joy or trial is from Heaven. That which burns and that which blows has its source in Heaven. Heaven's wind and Heaven's fire.

(b) Bankruptcy struck, without there being a Stock Exchange!

The fire of God had fallen and had burned up the sheep and the shepherds with them. A greater catastrophe is now upon him...where can he take shelter? What will he do in the dilemma? He takes refuge under the Everlasting wings and he finds that underneath are the Everlasting arms (Deuteronomy 33:27)! He moves near to God. "God is a very present help in trouble" (Psalms 46:1). He is more present than the trouble! The Egyptians believed that fire was an animal. It had sprung onto Job's sheep and burned them up. Job was never moved by the happenings of the day...Job 1:20...the loss of wealth stirred him little, but when he heard that the family had been carried off, this moved him profoundly. He tore his mantle — and he worshipped God. Tearing his mantle as if he was letting his heart out to worship...what a lovely disposition! It brought him to worship the God he loved. It brought his heart to offer its incense. It discovered the real God of his life. What a man is when he is on his back, and what a man is when he is on his knees before God, that is the measure of the man. The mouth is never the measure of the man. His manliness is seen and measured in the way he accepts adversity. Job fell at the feet not of valuables — there was no altar formed out of the treasures. He did not fall at the feet of the sheep or cattle, barns or bairns, fields or ploughs, but at the feet of God. How different from the rich young ruler who met with Jesus and went away sorrowful when he was challenged over his riches (Luke 18:23). Job realised the nakedness of life (Job 1:21). Life does not clothe us with the things which shall be. The things we see are only temporal. It is the things of the spirit which are unseen which are Eternal. Stripped of armour the finest warrior is but a man. Stripped, the most spiritual and the most saintly are but worshippers at the feet of God. Listen to what Job says in worship, words of such profound depth..."Naked I came out of my mother's womb, and naked I will return unto the earth" (Job 1:21). When we are in our birthday suit, that is the measure of mankind. As James exhorts us, we must "count it all joy when you fall into diverse temptations" (James 1:2). "The trials of many kinds" — Peter says (1 Peter 1:6 N.I.V.). These temptations could not be more diverse...blessed be the Name of Jehovah! Job throws himself onto the large mercy of the covenant keeping God. Job 1:11, according to the powers of darkness Job should by now be cursing God to His face. How wrong they can be! How wrong they are! They suspect our motives to be as damned as they are. To the impure all things are impure! How right God was! How splendid Job appears as this defeat is turned into triumph! These two impostors of pain and suffering are treated alike. Losing or winning doesn't matter, it is how we played the game. Job didn't charge God foolishly. He didn't lay the blame at God's feet. He laid himself there. May God give us strength to allow the feet of God to be placed upon us. We need grace to bear the weight of that which is allowed.

There is much more to come, as Satan, who commenced in the open field, went into the farmyard, then into the house to touch the family, now stoops to touch the body of Job. The trial comes ever closer.

(c) The affliction of his body

All that a man has will he give for his skin — so is the unreasonable reasoning of Satan (Job 2:4). God takes up that accusation as a Q.C. at the Bar, and He disproves it before the eyes of all. God proves, through Job, that life, deep eternal spiritual life, is more than flesh, blood or bone. God proves that hope is greater than body, faith is more firm, love is deeper and stronger than the flesh which surrounds us. Eye for an eye, tooth for a tooth, skin for skin a man will exchange one for another. Job might give skin for skin, but he would not give up God for suffering, wealth, family, sheep, oxen or fields! Job has greater wealth and possessions in his heart. He has them where nothing can break through and steal, not even affliction.

He was so smitten with boils that no unmarked place remained on his body. He had to scrape himself with a piece of broken pot, to remove all the pus and the slimy filth (Job 2:8). Every boil head was a fountain of filth. By his actions he is scraping away something far more vile. He is removing accusation and defeat. The image of God and the integrity of Job remained. They could not be scraped away with a bit of pottery. These are the important things of life...things of an Eternal nature which cannot be touched by sickness, which cannot destroy the soul, only the body. That which cannot be fallen on from above cannot be touched by sickness or disease, it cannot be shot down in flight. These are the choice treasures of the spirit of a man, that inner man which grows day by day, that inner man which produces through the light affliction a more exceeding weight of glory (2 Corinthians 4:17).

(d) The objections of his wife

Even Job's wife takes up the case of the opposition: "Curse God and die" (Job 2:9). Eat, drink and be merry, for tomorrow we die! Job 1:11 — she tells Job to "curse" God — yet she does not mean blaspheme. The word "curse" means "to bid God farewell". Give it up! Let it go! Why bother believing, what has it done for you? The wife may present the world's attitude to sickness, death and burial. Job, in answer, makes a remarkable statement. "Shall we not serve a two handed God?" (Job 2:10). Unlike a god with only one hand or who slumbers and sleeps. A God who is well balanced. Shall we not receive good and evil? The good overcoming the evil. We must have the sunshine and the shadows, the frost, the storms, as well as the happy days. He shall be my God, as the title of this book declares *In Sickness and In Health*. Make Him the God of it all, He is the all-round God with an all-round ministry of capability into misery. Misery and mystery can be marginalised through God.

Throughout the Book of Job you will find that God is watching. He is hiding in every page, marking the steps of Job (Job 32:11). God is speaking and controlling. He is never far from tragedy. He is never far from debate. He stands with us in discouragement. Whatever happens, comes from the hand of God and like the bread which Jesus broke, it has the markings of God upon it (Luke 22:19; Matthew 14:19). When you have been broken, blessed and divided there will still be twelve baskets left over!

Life is more valuable than family possessions or anything else, great or small. As the body is more than clothes, so the spirit of man is more than the man. We are attacked inwardly just as we are attacked outwardly. There are certain things in life and about life that you can measure. There are certain Eternal things such as faith, trust and integrity which can never be measured.

(e) The misunderstanding by his friends

This is another temptation which will try us many times as we mix freely with those around us. We meant it for good, they took it for bad. We tried to help, they thought we were interfering.

Job's comforters are world famous! Every family has them. You will find them in every part of society. They were supposed to be coming to help Job out of the mud and the mire, but all they succeeded in doing was to push him further into it. They are born pessimists, bringing the shadowy, foggy side of life to your already gloomy existence. These friends are coffin screws and gravediggers' spades! Their words to Job simply pushed him further into the storm. As with Jonah, they took him and threw him into the mouth of the storm (Jonah 1:12, 15). They were like the Egypt they represented, which is described as a reed (Isaiah 36:6). Lean on it, and there is a breaking. Part of it will go into your hand, causing injury. Strong human argument is never at the mercy of integrity or faith.

Job's friends are Eliphaz, Bildad and Zophar. Their conversations are contained in Chapters 4 — 14, Eliphaz; Chapters 15 — 21, Bildad; Chapters 22 — 31, Zophar. Elihud comes in at the end, rather like a parrot on a perch. He says a lot but doesn't add up to much. They had heard of Job's losses, but they didn't expect to find him so afflicted. They were like human reasoning which goes round in circles and meets itself coming back. They had no real answer to the problem of suffering. Their arguments and what they had to offer contains all the philosophies of this natural world. A sort of Darwin trip into evolution, made up of human imagination and thinking. It is the approach to sickness through the natural mind. It was not enough. It was incomplete. It was only a fragment of the whole which they brought with them. Thank God for the writer of the Book of Job. He has the full story...not the ending only, or the beginning, but the bits in-between as well! To give a full understanding of suffering you need the Book of Job, the whole Bible and the God of the Bible to make it all relevant.

God uses the friends, just as He uses Job, to provide answers for those listening in to their conversation in future generations. The Book of Job should be placed alongside the Bible in every hospital ward. The reasonable explanation which suffering cries out for is provided, not by Job's friends, but by Job himself. Argument after argument is presented and defeated like soldiers in a great battle. They are lain on one side, mortally wounded, with Job being crowned as the victor in every part. What "friends" have said and how they see things is superseded by a greater voice and vision — God and His Word.

Their theology was simply that Job had sinned, that there was rebellion in his life. Their theology stated that a good man is not made sick (Job 4:7, 8). Job must have been an unfaithful hypocrite, trying to justify himself before God, and no man could do that. He had tried to rise up and stand alongside God, and God had beaten him down into the ground. Now here he was, bleeding and dying. The marks of the Almighty were spread across his naked body. The friends were so persuasive — similar to some modern day preachers and doctrines. Job thought they might be right — but he only thought that for one moment. God stepped into the circle of argument and testified on Job's behalf (Job 1:8; 42:7, 9).

Eliphaz brings to us the voice of vision. God visited him in varying forms so therefore what Eliphaz says must be right. He has seen a thing or two. Knowledge comes with age and visions. He peered into the dark things. He knew all the answers. He was the answer even before the questions were asked! He had heard voices and communicated with the spirits of the unseen world. He was probably the oldest of the three.

Bildad comes with the knowledge of discovery. He has been around. He has sailed and travelled a little bit. He comes like the voyager with his ladened ship, to unload his wares. What he has discovered brings the answer to human suffering. Those who travel, know. Those who have mixed with the world have all the answers. Life has given him the right to answer every question on sickness. We have met the "friends" of Job, even in our own Churches. What Bildad has to say sheds no light on the problem. It deepens the darkness into blackest midnight, the sort of darkness which blows out candles! He is a man of theories.

Zophar does not rely on what the other two have been saying. He is of an individual and independent spirit. He makes up his own mind about these matters. He is the voice of reality — "of course, Job, you have sinned. We can see that from your boils. They are the initial evidence of sin" (Job 11:3, 4, 13, 14, 20). He brings no new thoughts or revelation about sickness. His message is: You are sick, make the best of it. Face the facts, i.e. lie down and die. The fact that all his ideas are homespun, doesn't matter to him. He believes it, so it must be right. Some religions of our day are like this...they believe certain things but they don't really know why they believe them. To Job they are like trees that don't give shade, leaf or sap. When the heat is on, the shade is denied. You need friends like this, as much as you need a hole in the head!

Job relied on their sympathy, but like Jesus when He came to the fig tree expecting fruit, he found none (Matthew 21:19).

Even Job's wife was ready to believe them. She succumbed to

their pressures. There was a God, but it was "friends" who were standing by Job. "Believe those things you see and act upon them." Curse God and die (Job 2:9). Believe God and live. This is what the Bible teaches. Trust God more and more and the Judge of all the earth shall do right. The God Who was in Jesus getting to know all about us. See the hand of God drawing back the curtain of blindness, darkness, heaviness, allowing understanding of suffering to shine right into the darkness. The darkness comprehends it not. Your suffering is completed in Jesus Christ. He suffered but was without sin. No guile was found in his mouth (1 Peter 2:22; 3:10). As the sheep is dumb before her shearers, so He opened not His mouth (Isaiah 53:7). There was no admixture in that which He said or that which He did. Even Pilate said, "I find no fault in Him".

The friends of Job are still alive

D.L.Moody said, 'These three friends of Job, they are typical of natural ability which tried to restore Job, a Job who had never fallen".

They argued from the point of view that it had happened because of what was wrong with Job. They never saw it as happening because of what was wrong with Satan. They never saw it as happening because of the righteousness of God. They never saw, they never knew, they could never understand what we understand because of what the New Testament reveals to us. They saw through a glass darkly. It was riddled with holes, casting distorted shadows as they gazed into it. They were judgemental in the extreme and they did not, could not, help Job in his suffering. They caused him even further wounds and pain.

There are disciples, alive and well today, who are Job's friends. They will tell you to snap out of it. They say, "If you had been in the will of God this would not have happened. You should have trusted God more. You tried to do it in your own strength!" Empty blasts of a trumpet are these, and no walls fall down when they sound their unmusical notes. It does not help to criticise those who are ill or burdened with some tragedy, particularly if they are suffering in some way in which we have never suffered. It is easy to tell the man who has fallen down a mountain that he should never have climbed it in the first place, especially if we have never accepted the challenge. Peter did walk on water, although he began to sink (Matthew 14:28). None of the other disciples accomplished that.

There have been some cases of mistaken identity, of totally misunderstanding suffering. Mental illness is still a leprosy in modern society. There are those who will always have all the answers. The answers they give create even more questions and become a breeding ground for doubt and fear. You are not bettered, but battered by these. Even the "Home Doctor" does not give the answers we require.

God will only let argument and debate continue for so long, then He will step in. Heaven will be God's final Word on all things, the last anthem to our suffering. No more curse, sorrow, crying, night or pain (Revelation 21:4). That which has been in part shall be made perfect. That which is Perfect is going to come. We shall then know even as we are known (1 Corinthians 13:12).

If at the end or edge of a bed of sickness or from beneath a burden at its heaviest the sufferer can cry with great conviction the words: "I know that 'my' Redeemer lives!" (Job 19:25), they will be as medicine indeed to all who hear and accept them. They will come forth as gold which has been tried in the fire, and which did not waste away. They will gain a new lustre, a new brilliance, shining into the lives of others. Men will rise up from all walks of life and from every generation as a mixed multitude whose gelling factor has been suffering and pain, and they will call you blessed.

NOTE

1. Doctor Adam Clarke was an early Methodist commentator. He has written a Bible commentary.

CHAPTER

3

Understanding your suffering

*If only I knew where to find him: if only I could go to his
dwelling! I would state my case before him and fill my mouth
with arguments. I would find out what he would answer me and
consider what he would say. (Job 23:3 - 5, N.I.V.)*

*Neither is there any umpire between us, that he might lay his
hand on both of us. (Job 9:33, R.S.V.)*

In the suffering of sickness or some other form of suffering is
there anyone who understands? We know there is through the
Patience of Job. We know from the previous chapter, just what
God is looking for in that which he allows. If God allows it, then
receive it, "Count it all joy", says the apostle James.

Job was asking for a man to understand him, and represent him.
In this chapter there is the discovery of a Yakach, an umpire. To
know that God knows, and that our representative is at His right
hand, switches on every light, and it turns up every dim light which
might have been going out. We are understood and we begin to
understand what we are passing through.

The Jesus Christ of the New Testament answers the question and
plea of Job. That same Jesus, this same Jesus is the answer to every
question. Suffering can seem to snatch at our sensibilities, and we
tend to lose our direction as a careering wheel, free from its axle.
The truth, the very truth we believe can become discordant and distorted. The straight steel pin can become a screw. We are often left
looking for One with understanding and compassion. As believers,
we know a Man who can and does what he has promised.

*   *   *

There was a deep longing in the soul of Job for someone who would rightly represent God and the people, bringing them together in understanding and they, being understood, would be at ease with themselves and with God. We need to know that in the deep darkness there is a God Who understands us through Jesus Christ and all He accomplished through the Cross. Jesus in all His mediatorial work getting to know mankind forever. To know that He is flesh, blood and spirit, even as we are. To know there is One Who is in the shades of suffering with us, staying with us, praying for us, caring, strengthening. One Who appears at the right Hand of God on our behalf (1 John 2:1; Romans 8:27, 34; Hebrews 7:25), as we pass through the Valley of the Shadow of Death.

The hands of Jesus, so large, so strong, takes hold of two ends and two natures blending them, so that you cannot tell where one commences and another concludes. One Who could understand both man and God, Who would have to be God and man, equal with both and yet surrendering nothing but having all things, allowing Him, the unique One, to be the representative of both. Having equal desire towards both, being for neither party exclusively but for both parties unanimously. One in whom all my hopes, fears and tears can freely find a place of rescue, where they all merge and are transformed. This is the Master Builder. The very work of Christ is to understand and to be understood by us.

Understanding the figures of life

Job, in the later verses of Chapter 9:25 and 26, sees life like a sailing ship. It can sink, it can be grounded on the rocks, it is subject to winds, storms and tides. It is a frail barque. Then he sees life as swift as an eagle as it drops from the sky like a stone, heading for its prey. One moment there is life then, in an instant, death. One second there is nothing, the next we are held in cruel talons, pain tearing at us from every side. The days of man are as a ship sailing out of sight over the horizon. They are as swift as an eagle, hungrily bearing down on its prey. One minute there, the next gone without trace. If you have ever looked starboard from a sailing ship there is very little evidence of it having sailed across the water. It is the same when the eagle has carried off its prey. There is no history of the events. They have no progeny or genealogy. Job longs that the ship will sail forever and that the eagle's flight will remain forever, but how can that be? That is the vital question. The answer and all the answers are found in Jesus Christ. It is all possible if he can find an "umpire". The Hebrew word is *Yakach*, the judge, the daysman. There are certain ones who could and would present a good case before us for an individual cause. Some member of an elite club could make representation for that club. There might even be a pressure group involved. There might be an umpire for the rich, the poor, the sick, the wayward, the religious and even for Kings. What is required is one for all, and all for one. You could go through the whole fruit on a family tree and never find such a one among humans, and this is why Job utters this mocking cry. This is why, years later, at that first Christmas, God answered that cry with more than just an echo. Did Heaven hear that mocking cry? Did the King of Glory hear it and face the challenge like a David going out to do battle with Goliath? (1 Samuel 17:46). Was the answer despatched around Heaven in the words "Who will go for us, and whom shall we send?" (Isaiah 6:8).

Life is a battle. Life is a game. It is a sail, it is a wing, it is a flight. It is that for which we need an umpire. One who will bring together all parties concerned, correctly and with understanding. During my sickness in the heat of the battle when all around me is shaken, when the ground of my confidence wobbles then, like Job, I need One Who understands me as a man, One who can bring me to God, Who can arrest me by His capabilities and lay me not simply in a hospital bed, but lay me down to sleep in peace (Psalm 4:8).

The requirement to be understood, and to understand

The cry for a *Yakach* has trumpeted from his lips because of the woeful inadequacies of one party — mankind — and the inability we have to understand ourselves let alone the immensity of God. We go through life simply saying "I am fearfully and wonderfully made" (Psalm 139:14).

There has never been a man after the stamp of Adam who could also bear the image of God, other than Jesus Christ (Romans 5:10, 11, 14, 15, 21). There was never one man who could claim the heart and the ear of God when presenting our case before Him. A doctor, a lawyer, a probation officer, psychiatrist, social worker, sick visitor and Minister all rolled into one, moulded into one likeness performing great deeds for mankind. No one could claim to have the whole heart of God, let alone the throbbing, sick, bleeding and dying heart of mankind. No man cared for my soul. Not one person with arched back over troubled waters. There was no bridge-builder between God and man. The gap was too great, the leap too short. We always tried to reach God at the widest point, failing to touch Him, faltering in our reach. The nearer we came to God, the greater the restrictions and the gap. We were made to feel unclean, unworthy, unholy, because God was unapproachable. Approaching God was like putting a hand into nettles or a bee hive. The same cry of Job was uttered through the lips of every tribe, tongue and nation, year after year and epoch after epoch, yet it only seemed to reach to the clouds and reverberate. The yearning, hoping, pleading was like a stone skimmed on the surface of a lake, appearing for a time, rising a few inches giving us hope that it might continue, only to plunge to the inky depths as it sped away.

The need to know that you are understood

There was such a need for a *Daysman*, the man of the day, the man who can help me in my calamity and visit me in my day of trouble (Job 9:33; 1 Timothy 2:5). Man, and yet God, with one hand on the shoulder of both parties drawing them into conversation and an established relationship. A substitute who would keep man together. The gap was so great, as far as the east is from the west and the earth is from Heaven. We must not just stand together or be placed together, we must stay together for ever, an Eternal stand and standing. Not as that which is forced into unity, but blended as nature with nature, of the same sequence and stock. Humanly, to obtain a Daysman, one would require to be born into a family, be adopted into another family, return to the original family to marry, only then might he understand both parties. To bring rags and riches, to unite royalty with rags, you need a prince who is dressed in rags. He must be a beggar from the dunghill, as well as the prince from the palace. The person needed in Job's suffering had to be one hundred percent with both parties. He must not be mongrel or hybrid, he must not be centaur, half man and half beast. Job was sobbing for one to come and stand with him, to help him in his time of need, one who could tell him and show him where God was in all the mess, so that from the tangled web, silk might be spun. He had to come to Job's side without leaving God's side. He had to be with Job and yet be with God. He had to be one with both, to be a true Daysman. Where could such a one be found? You could send throughout the kingdom, just like King Ahasuerus did in the Book of Esther (Esther 1:19; 2:2), looking for a fair virgin, and still not find the one the New Testament calls the Answer (Revelation 3:14).

The provision of that understanding

Could those who carve images out of wood and stone provide such a one, for it is the cry of the whole tribe of Adam on this terrestrial ball? Could Noah, that renowned carpenter, build one? Could Abraham, that possessor of foreign lands, claim one? Those who work in stone, slate, silver, maybe they could shape such a one? Dear Bezaleel, the first worker in brass and iron, please shape a Daysman! He could not. The end product would be a graven image. The finest Master Builders have no blueprint and, therefore, become bunglers. Could it be accomplished by inter-breeding, through some genetic force? He must not be half God and half man. He must be one hundred percent God and one hundred percent man. He has to be Very God of Very God and Very Man of Very Man. Not a demi-god, not fifty percent of both man and God, but a hundred percent of both. Nothing must be surrendered in bringing them together. No ground must be given or taken from each party involved.

The old American Indians used to have a very cunning trick which worked well when they wanted to get amongst a herd of buffalo in order to kill one. They would dress in the skin of a dead buffalo and pretend to be such an animal, in order to get near to the herd without causing a stampede. A little like our shepherds. When a lamb dies or the mother of a lamb rejects its young, they take the skin off the dead lamb and put it over the living one, so that the mother adopts it as its own. Isaac knew that the hands he held were those of Jacob, but it was the voice of Esau (Genesis 27:22). No matter how well the wife of Jeroboam was disguised, the Prophet of Israel saw through the disguise and recognised her (1 Kings 14:6).

Jesus Christ provides that understanding

All the eyes of the world will be upon the Daysman. He must be what he says he is. He must be examined and found to be real. He will be tested as no other. The Refiner of silver will sit and gaze at his life. He must stay under the gaze of the scrutineers for thirty three years until one who lived near to Him writes: *"In Him was no guile"* (1 Peter 2:22).

Life can be so cruel, so frustrating when we do not know or do not feel that we have a representative with God. Someone who can translate pain into peace and torment into tumultuous triumph, rather as our Ombudsman deals with complaints. We need one to decide between right and wrong. Someone to tell me when I am wrong and to cover that wrong, making it as if it had never happened. Someone God can lay claim to and man can lay claim to. It is one who can rebuke, reprove, exhort, and comfort with all authority. This is the meaning of *Yakach*, the Hebrew word translated "daysman" in the King James version and "umpire" in other versions. It is from a root word according to Dr. Strong[1] which means "to be right" — to be right and fair, seeing, knowing, experiencing from every angle. It is Jesus on Jesus, the Son of Man and the Son of God. Mankind was far from God. We needed a path, a light, an open door to Him.

The long-suffering of Job has not only to be right but it must be declared right with authority by a Daysman who understands God and men. One who understands me as an individual. The Patriarchs traversed the Promised Land looking for an advocate, a Daysman who would be their representative before God, before a God who was just, holy, pure and far removed. They needed someone to take hold of the hand of God and the hand of men and join the two hands together for always. A person of two natures, from two camps, two areas yet leading to one destination. A person of two natures who could lift his hand and declare whether we were in or out, rejected or accepted by each party. One who brings in the Law and Grace. They tried Abraham with all his qualities. They tried Moses, Joshua, even the Levitical Priesthood was brought in to help, but all had a shortness that would not reach.

We are in need of a great *Yakach*. There is a great gulf fixed throughout the Old Testament between a Holy God and sinful men. Who will be the bridge over troubled waters? Who will be some great Brunel and build for us an iron bridge a way back to the heart of God? Who will have love of such a stretch and so great dimensions?

The one appointed of God understands you

Genesis 24:14, 44 — we have the same thought of the Daysman brought out in this text. What is concealed is revealed for us. A bride is being sought for Isaac. "Let this be the one you have 'appointed'. The one my master has 'appointed'." This one was to bring two separated families together. There was to be a wedding, an arranged meeting. One from each area, camp and place had to meet through a mediator. Genesis 31:35, 42, the word Yakach describes Laban look-ing through the belongings of Jacob...seeking, looking, "seeking to ascertain" what is there. It is the idea of judgement through seeking.

Genesis 31:24. Again, the same thought. "See that you speak neither good or bad." Suspend your judgement of him. God has longed to do this for ages. When God sees the Cross, the suffering pain of Jesus then, God says, "I will pass over you. I will become lame. My judgement will fall short, because of blood shed. I will not see what I can see. I will not know what I know. My judgement will never reach as far as you."

The understanding of all parties

The A.S.V. and the R.S.V. gives the meaning of *Yakach* as "umpire" (Job 9:33). In the raising of the hand the decision was made. There needs to be an umpire between us and our great God. The raising of the hand by the umpire meant a covenant was ratified. Both parties must do it, and both did, in Jesus being God and man. The hands of Jesus were raised on the Cross as a witness. One who is flesh of my flesh, bone of my bone, spirit of my spirit, very man of very man needs to be appointed by both parties. The person who stands there must understand my feebleness, the frailty of man. He must know my emotions through and through. The lot of mankind must have flowed through his veins as a river in full flood. He must know what it is to be both red in tooth and claw. Isaiah takes the thought a step forward in his promises, prophecies and precepts in the direction of reconciliation when he says, "Come let us reason together" (Isaiah 1:18). Let us debate our case in a Law Court. God has no case to answer, but what about us? What about little me, arrayed against a great God and Judge? The stick versus the mountain, the gnat trying to outfly the eagle! Wait! Your representative in this matter is going to be no less than God Himself in the Person of Jesus Christ! (Hebrews 1:3).

The case for good is wholesome and God has nothing to answer for. The evidence is on His side and the case is weighted against us. Who will tip the scales of justice and judgement in our favour? I have found a man! Jesus steps on to our side and into our shoes as a man and brings about an equilibrium. The scales are balanced between justice, judgement, wrath, mercy, love and forgiveness. Demand and payment are met in One.

Tyndale, commenting on Exodus 21:22, says, "He shall pay as a Daysman appoints". I have nothing to pay to him who is saying Pay me what you owe me! I cannot bottom the depths of God's asking. There is no measure with which to measure His standards.

The Book of Genesis illustrates that if we sin we can make an offering as prescribed by God for that sin, but it will never bring the outstretched hands together. Exodus, Leviticus, Deuteronomy repeat the same pattern, a Holy God who cannot be approached, and sinful man who would approach but who is too sinful and therefore too distasteful. Bringing the two together is like snow to fire. In the Book of Judges if a man wrongs God, he can go to Eli. Each book of the Bible presents a system, but it is weak, it is old, it decays, removed for ever by a new and a Living Way in Jesus Christ, in Whom are hid all the treasures of wisdom, knowledge and riches of grace.

Being heard and fully understood

Who was a Daysman? He was man for the day! The man who appoints a day for the case to be heard.[2] The word Daysman, in the English language is from "dais-man", the man who sits on the dais, a raised table at the end of a room where the judge sat and passed sentence. Our sentence was passed onto Christ! He, the just, suffered for the unjust. 1 Timothy 2:5 ... "there is one God and Mediator between God and man, the man Christ Jesus". That phrase meets the needs of all parties. What Job could only long for, we have in Jesus Christ. We have One in the presence of God for us. Our Umpire, our Daysman, our Representative is Jesus Christ Who had been tempted in all points, Who has suffered (Hebrews 4:15). He has known the Holiness of God and the humanity of man. As in the story of David and Jonathan who were knit together, Jonathan the King's son placed his garments and weapons upon David, the shepherd lad (1 Samuel 18:1, 4).

Dr. John Gill[3] in his Commentary on the Bible provides us with some thoughts on the Daysman. "The custom amongst the Arabs for appointing a daysman was probably borrowed from the Hebrew nation. One representing both parties stands in the middle of the two. He takes both their hands and cuts the large finger, the index finger, with a sharp stone. Then he took a piece of material from both their garments, dipped the torn pieces in the blood which had been shed, sprinkling seven stones erected as witnesses as an altar between them. Whilst doing this he would pray to his deity. Both parties are thus reconciled. They embrace, then join together at a feast with friends."

The ministry of Jesus is to understand your misery

When Jesus died the Hand of God took the hand of humanity, grasping it tightly forever, as if He was the miser and we were the money. That is why a body was prepared for Jesus Christ. God was pained and cut by our sin in Jesus. He must have a body for that to happen. The Septuagint translates our text in Job 9 v 33. *"O that there was a Mediator between us." There is! There is! There is! Such a One has been found! He is rarer than the rarest, the fairest of the sons of men, like the gold of Ophir and the balm of Gilead.* In fact He has come to us — Galatians 3:19 — "By the hands of a Mediator." Hebrews 8:6, 9:15, 15:12, 24. Jesus was the Hand of God. "If I by the finger of God cast out devils" — Luke 11:20. God spilled His blood on the Cross for our sins and our sicknesses. God, in Jesus, shed His blood. Christ as a man shed human blood for us. That piece of garment which belonged to God, a Holy God, was dipped in rich red blood. That piece of garment which was our filthy rags was dipped in His fountain of blood. Our index fingers, which point so much and are so active, had to be cut, put out of joint, so that Jesus might reset them in the right direction to grasp the important things of life and point the way to God. We came together with clenched fists, but Jesus, through His love, prized them open to embrace. Jesus has torn the image of God and man forever. He has presented one whole new man. God has been seen in another form. As Stanley Jones used to say, "If God is not like Jesus, I don't want to know Him." Jesus had torn the veil, unwrapping God forever (Matthew 27:51). A way through that which had surrounded God has been found in Jesus (Hebrews 10:20). Through the torn flesh of Jesus (Hebrews 10:20), God has been able to step into every situation. If the sun cannot get through, God can! God, known for ourselves. The old religion had been torn into pieces and placed on one side for ever. What God and men have been hiding behind has been lifted away, torn from top to bottom for always. That white linen fence around the Tabernacle has been removed in Christ. God and man are in perfect harmony. One is the tune, the other is the song.

As the Arab or the Hebrew performed the reconciliation ceremony, he called upon his deity. Jesus Himself cried, "Forgive them, for they know not what they do" (Luke 23:34). There is an Advocate with the Father, Jesus Christ the Righteous. *"He makes intercession for the transgressors"* (Isaiah 53:12). God accepts you as He would accept Jesus. You are like a jewel which cannot be counted for worth. The jewel and the brass buckle on the shoe are equally acceptable because they are on the person who is present. We are accepted in the Beloved! Child of God, have no fear! You are as accepted as the nearest to the heart of God! Through Jesus you have been made into one of God's heartbeats. He loves you because there is no other you. You are uniquely loved because you are unique.

As in the Greek fable of Adonis, there are fair flowers which have sprung up from the blood of Christ. We are like the almshouses which Dr. Barnardo first purchased to help people. Each house was named after a flower.

Jesus in understanding us unites us to God

Romans 7 and 8 present to us the seven witnesses of our reconciliation: 7:25, deliverance from sin; 8:2, Spirit of Christ; 8:3, 4, righteousness; 8:5, 6, a mind for the things of the Spirit is peace; 8:9, 10, Christ in us; 8:14, led by the Spirit of God; 8:16, the Spirit bearing witness unto sonship. The spirit *bears witness* with our spirit that we are born of God. He *bears witness* as a witness in a Court of Law agrees with the statement we have made. There is far more evidence for us than anything which was against us. If God be for us, who can be against us? The Daysman had to point out all the relevant details of oneness between the parties. There was no oneness, there were no relevant details without Jesus Christ supplying them through the Cross on our behalf. Thanks be to God for His unspeakable Gift! We say that a man's gift makes room for him. That is true, but also God's gift, in John 3:16, makes room for God. This is how much God understands us, and this is how we understand Him, through Jesus Christ. Philip said, *"Show me the Father and that will be enough."* N.I.V.. *"Have I been so long with you, Philip, and have you not known me? He that has seen Me has seen the Father also."* (John 14:8, 9, N.I.V.).

What a work it was! All the unholy deeds which were in the hands of men fell out of those hands as we were brought with open hand, the Hand that was nailed to the Cross for us. My hand, your hand, all our hands joined to the Hand of God in Jesus Christ. That means the finger of God is in my life. God the Son meeting the sons of God and making them one with God, just as if they had never sinned!

When the Daysman placed his hand on both parties it revealed that he had authority with them both. They both accepted him bringing them together. Jesus more than took our hands — He took our whole humanity to that Cross.

I have found myself a Daysman! 1 Corinthians 4:3, the word "judgement" is given elsewhere as "day" (Matthew 6:34; Mark 6:11). The Daysman is the one who has judged for us. The Christ of our day, for our times, for our sins and for our sickness.

The very term used for salvation, *soteria*, is used in Romans 1:16; Luke 1:69. It is given as *health* in Acts 27:34. It is rescue and mercy. It is to save from perishing in every part of life and living. It is deliverance which takes many forms and is multi-faceted in Jesus Christ.

Mediator means going between — whatever the cost, to go between. Having run the gauntlet He brings us together, our Mediator. We owe nothing to God. We owe nothing to the love of God. We owe nothing to justice, mercy, holiness, wrath or any other claim of God. All the claims are fully met in Jesus.

> "I owed a debt I could not pay,
> He paid a debt He did not owe."

He has taken away the handwriting of ordinances which were against us and nailed them to His Cross (Colossians 2:14). We have a Referee Who has blown the whistle on every foul deed, every action which was against the Book of Rules, the Law of God, the Holy commands of God have all been settled in full. Jesus, as Daysman, was not the down payment but the Payment in Full! He wasn't "something on account" — He was the full amount of payment for salvation and healing (John 19:30).

Understanding that God is all knowing and all caring

From the root of this word *Yakach* we have the thought of daylight and sunshine. Jesus has brought us out of the shade and into the brilliant sunshine of full revelation because He is the Light of the World, and whoever follows Him shall not walk around in the darkness but shall have the Light of Life. Not a flicker of hope only, but a fulness. From the Daysman we have the Daystar and the Dayspring. Luke 1:78 The Dayspring, the springing of a new day. The day of grace, the age of an ageless, classless and endless Church. Look at the Daysman and you will see the replica of both parties — the Son of God and the Son of Man.

In Matthew 2:2, the word "Dayspring" is usually translated "the east". The place from whence the sun arises to begin its journey through another day, transforming everything by its beautiful rays, saying to this flower "bloom", to this tree "bud", to this rain, "drop, follow Me!" Calling those out of darkness and sleep. Transforming the landscape into a variety of colours when all has been clothed in darkness.

All that which Jesus has accomplished should bring us to the place of the fabled Anacreon's harp which, we are told, could only play one tune. It was wedded to that one tune for ever. Only one song was ever sung from it. Jesus is the One Song, the vibrant note, the great universal theme. There is One Name, One Word, One Note as we rise in adoration to worship Him.

Even from our blind sickness, our great trials, the battlefield is large and the wounds are many, but because we are built on the Rock nothing is taken from us. Trials and difficulties only add to us. God's medicine comes in many bottles and many hands can administer, sometimes for a sudden healing, other times a slow process.

All come through the Mediator of a "better" covenant, based on "better" promises, through a "better" way (Hebrews 7:19, 22; 8:6; 9:23), to make me into a better person, spiritually, physically, morally, emotionally and eternally! In all this that I might be understood and that I also might understand.

NOTES

1. Dr. James Strong, S.T.D., L.L.D., Exhaustive Concordance: Dictionary of Hebrew and Greek Words (Baker Book House, Grand Rapids, Michigan).

2. See Chambers original dictionary.

3. Dr. John Gill, D.D.. Puritan commentator born in Kettering, Northamptonshire. The quote is from his commentary on the whole Bible.

CHAPTER
4

The Suffering Servant

Jesus knew sorrow in its fullest measure. Ours will always be the pin prick, while he suffered the real pain. He was crowned with a crown of hurting, piercing thorns. Being afflicted, and being in agony makes him one with us. This gives meaning to the previous chapter on understanding. My heart beat echoes in His heart beat. What I feel, He feels, because what I am He became. In the pain of his understanding, through his sufferings, I begin to understand that He does.

What is my suffering when compared with his cross. My sighs and aches are but few when compared with the army of his assailants. Yet, it is that suffering which brings my Shepherd into the sheepfold. He was a Man, and a Man of Sorrows. He is a Doctor to the disabled. The Surgeon of the suffering. You will discover for yourself in the next few minutes a Christ who had his feet fixed on earth, and cared enough to cry with compassion.

❋   ❋   ❋

The Kings of old had their Court Jesters. Cards must always have jokers concealed within the pack. There was no room for sorrow with the Romans or Greeks. The old liturgy made the point, re-sharpening it every time the words were uttered in worship or used as a statement of belief in the Creed, for the Greek liturgy stated, "Thine unknown suffering". Here was the darkness without the day, and the deepest darkness at that, where no moon or star was visible. That which Jesus passed through was as it was in the judgement of Egypt, darkness which could be felt.

The depth and the darkness of the sufferings of Jesus Christ can never be fully known. We have only passing glimpses of His

sufferings and agonies as, allowed by Holy Writ, we glance at Him
but for a moment at the midnight hour.

Jesus was the suffering Saviour

We know that Jesus was a Man of eloquence, for "no man spake like
this man" (Luke 4:36; Matthew 7:29). We know He was a Man of
miracles: we acknowledge that He was a Man of wisdom: He was a
Man of zeal, for it was upon Him as a cloak (John 2:17); He was a
Man of intensity. Here was a Man Who possessed human traits in
their fulness. He was no wimp, no soft option. Jesus was a Man
Who could face great odds, and win! He was never a figure cast in
bronze, formed in marble or moulded into clay. He was a Man of
Galilee, but when we study, watch and mark Him as a suffering
Saviour it is then that our words begin to stutter and what I want to
say stays in my mouth, turned as it were to stone.

Beginning as a Babe in obscurity He grew in wisdom and favour
both with God and with man. He rose to be a strong Man and at the
end of His suffering He was and shall ever remain head and shoulders above everyone else, with a strong hand to lift and help us, with
strong feet to lead the way through all endeavours which would limit
and hold us back (Philippians 2:9, 10). He has a glow in His eyes
which penetrates all the darkness of the night. His voice has such a
steel ring about it that demons flee at one word of command from
Him. I must walk in the shadow of this One to find that in Him I
have a friend of the universe and a universal Friend. It would be far
easier to accept Jesus as a Man of joy, peace, love, goodness, kindness. He was all of these, and more. Around His neck hang the
pearls of suffering. He had to enter within that dark vale for all of us
and, after suffering, bring many sons to glory.

I can fully understand a person suffering, but not the Person of
Jesus Christ.

The depths of His unknown sufferings

The Greeks and Romans had no god which would express suffering
in all its reality. They were not allowed to enter into the presence of

the King with a dull sour face, a face which looked as if it had lost all life and form, a face which was an expression of depression, as if sadness and being forlorn had made its secret abode there. They were not meant to suffer, but to rejoice, to rent a house only on the sunny side of the street. Everything must be green and rosy in the garden and birds must constantly sing. We know that life can never be like that. Sometimes the sun goes in and the clouds gather. We become as Pilate, whose original name according to W. Barclay[1] means "cloud-capped". We can never be as the sun dial on which was written "I only record the sunny hours". There must be storms and we have to face them. No ship worth its timber can stay in port forever and a day. The hour must come when it feels the breeze, when the timbers must be strained to be strengthened. The hour of its baptism has arrived, the salt must whip it and the waves must beat it, the anchor must limit and the Captain must command. It has to face the deep. So are the lives of everyone of us. Knowing that we have a Christ Who came and did not stand afar off, was not like the star which came, shone and stood where He was. We realise that angelic choirs may be alright on the night and for the occasion of the Birth of Jesus Christ, but there has to be that downward glance, that place where my foot touches the surface of all experiences where leather meets pavement.

Jesus recognises your suffering

The Bible states that He was a *"Man of Sorrows, acquainted with grief"* (Isaiah 53:3). It does not use the word "acquainted" as we would use it when referring to someone we do not really know. This use of the word "acquainted" is much more profound. It means, He fully understood and recognised grief, being part of it. It means to know fully by reason and experiment resulting in experience. It is the proving of a science that something works through experiment, through trial and on into triumph. In another tense it is translated "a person of skill and of knowledge — such as are skilful" (2 Chronicles 2:7, 14). 2 Chronicles 2:14 describes those who are skilful in silver and gold, those who make objects out of metals. A brooch is made, a ring for the finger is produced, or even a bracelet by their knowledge and a form or shape takes place from the metal. It describes a work in hard and resistant materials. Character is like metal. We can be a Barzillai who would not go all the way with King David (2 Samuel 19:34). His name means Stalin, the iron man. Habakkuk 2:14 describes the earth being "full of the knowledge of the Lord". The earth is God's workshop, His manual, His book of wisdom. Jesus is our Manual for living and triumphing over trials because of the knowledge that we have that He has been here also. Wherever you are in suffering and sickness, just like the story of Robinson Crusoe, you will find a footprint in the sand — someone else has been there. As they came to the tomb the Bible says *they saw the place where He lay* (Matthew 28:6). Jesus has marked suffering for ever. Where it was dark, He has placed a shining light so that we may see our way through and not falter. If you move to the right or the left, if you pass up or down, you will find the Son of Man standing somewhere in the shadows saying, "Do yourself no harm, we are all here" (Acts 16:28). The Son of Man showing the way to the Sons of God. Jesus is with you right now!

When a family needed someone to take care of their lame dog, they placed an advertisement in the newspaper. Many people applied, but one youngster came and, when he was asked what qualified him to look after the lame dog, he rolled up his trouser and revealed a steel brace on one of his legs. The boy was immediately chosen. Lame even as the dog was, he would have compassion and understanding.

Jesus undergirds our suffering

Jesus has limited Himself for us, that we might have confidence in His understanding of us. He understands humanity and our needs just as much as He understood carpentry or Creation. Fixing a wheel is just as important as fixing the heart. Mending a cart or a character, mending a shaft of a Son of God is part of His intervention.

I am cheered greatly when I begin to ask God to help with a problem or a sickness, or with a burden too great for me. God could have stood aloft, but the God of the stars and the God of Mars must become the God of the tea cup, the table, the chair and the bed, the common place, helping with common things, just as Martha wanted Mary to help her (Luke 10:40). Sadness can find its counterpart in Jesus Christ. Romans 8:26 — "He 'helps' our infirmities". The word "helps" is the same word used by Mary when she requested help from Martha in Luke 10:40. Jesus helps us in that way.

Here we have a God Who not only says, *Cast all your care on Me, for it matters to Me about you* (1 Peter 5:7). He has proved that it matters by being nailed to a Cross. He has not written it with a gold stemmed pen dipped in liquid gold for the few only — the Man of Sorrows covers the universe and claims universal sorrow of whatever nature for Himself. He deals with every sorrow irrespective of size, shape or shade. Whatever shakes you, He puts a foundation under, so that you wobble not.

The One we can turn to for help is a Man of Sorrows. He has gone through the veil of suffering, proving that He was a man and as a man He can approach us as man to man. He is a Man to help mankind. Jesus has entered physically into every area of suffering — eye for eye, tooth for tooth, skin for skin, every particle. He is hungry in everyone's hunger, sick in everyone's sickness, wanting in everyone's want and need, and thirsty when we thirst. That is why we can visit Him when He is sick and give Him to drink when He is thirsty, because as we do it unto others, we do it unto the Lord Christ.

Jesus became part of your pain

Whenever Jesus went to heal, help or give a word of advice He never simply sent messages with angels. When Jesus came, He came Himself, as Himself. To be Himself He had to become a man. He was the Messenger of God and the Message of God which deals with the problem of pain and perplexity. He sat where we sit. He has been and He has seen as we ourselves see. He knows as we know all the areas of life, whether it be in the duck pond or in the palace. He is a Man for all seasons. Many times the healing process is set in motion not by any action but by the fortitude which is bred in us, knowing that Jesus Christ is standing with us, that He too has been in a similar situation. To know that God, not sitting on a distant cloud or encased in an altar, candlestick, stained glass window, but God Who has walked the earth, Who has experienced joy and pain, is the One Who has promised to be near us, with us and help us in unseen ways. "I will never leave you nor forsake you" (Hebrews 13:5).

We are more than body, even as a garden is more than flowers, or water more than fish, we are body, soul and spirit and we need help in these three areas. Sometimes I only understand this when I am free from illness, when I have been given a clean bill of health. After the event I begin to piece the puzzle of happenings together and it is then that I understand there has been an unseen Hand at work in my life. It is only after the storm that I see the rainbow and the new shoots of green growth. Within every globule of rain there is another springtime. Then and only then do I appreciate the elaborate workings of God much more than I understand the workings of a machine or electricity. The situation had been altered by God pouring His grace through the Man of Sorrows into my sorrows. 1 Peter 4:10 N.I.V. "God's grace in its various forms." God making me so large that the bands are burst asunder. A God, in the Man of Sorrows Who causes me to grow big and strong. He is not too big to care and not too small to conquer!

The compassionate Christ consolidates suffering

Jesus doesn't say "Cheer up, laugh it off!" He knows that life is no skip, hop or jump. It is not a constant playtime. It is not clown shaped. The substance of what Jesus gives, its depth and height of help, is far more real and long lasting than that. His compassion went out to them. It doesn't wash off in the stormy weather or go overboard in times of storm. Many translations give it as "His heart went out to them" (Matthew 18:27), when speaking of the compassion of Christ. Sharing His heart with people, baring His soul in the Garden of Gethsemane, giving His hands and feet, yielding His time and place to the race that He came to save, the race which would leave Him behind and reject Him. The greatest thing about redemption and the plan of God, including all that Jesus began both to "do" and "teach" is not the beatitudes, those golden rules, as good as they are. It is not the mighty miracles, and they are powerful; it is not arising from the dead; it is the fact that I need Him in my need now. The God of the "how" becomes the God of the "now". It is in the fact that God can understand me...that as I pass through the valley there is One Who is walking through it with me. As in the Sands of Time I only recognise one set of footprints, forgetting that there was a time when God was carrying me!

Jesus is the Man of Sorrows in your suffering

Note...He is not a God of Sorrows — that would be unthinkable, unreal, untenable. He is a Man of Sorrows — flesh of my flesh and bone of my bone. He was Someone Who cared enough to cry over men, as with a trickle of tears on one occasion over a family and then with a great gushing of tears over the City of Jerusalem. Jesus not only cried for all, but He died for all! That liquid pain ran down His cheeks.

We can examine Jesus Christ with a better examination than the Romans or the Jews did at Gabbatha in the Judgement Hall (John 19:13). As we read the Gospels we see how He entered into every human emotion. We look not through a glass darkly but we see Him Face to face. The emotional vista is there. He was more than emotion, He passed through every human feeling — pain, joy, love, hatred, passion, laughter, tears — the whole season of human existence. The One Who shed tears also shed blood on the Cross. He knew what it was to be abandoned — "My God, My God, why have You forsaken Me?" (Mark 15:34). "He came unto His own and His own received Him not" (John 1:11). There was no place in their place for Jesus Christ. There was no room in the Inn. There was no room in the Palace. Even when He visited the house of Simon the Leper. There was no room for water in the wash bowl to wash the weary, dusty tired feet of Jesus — Luke 7:44. There was no room in the tide and affairs of men. The only place reserved for Him was on a Cross. Even the tomb did not have a place for Him. Jesus sleeps in an open boat (Mark 4:38; Matthew 5:1). He has to preach from mountain tops and from the roadside. When He wants transport He has to borrow a donkey. When He is thirsty He has to ask a woman of doubtful reputation to give Him a drink (John 4:7). He is one with outcasts, "down and outs" and those who have been cast out. He says to them: "Come unto Me all you who are weary and heavy laden and I will give you rest" (Matthew 11:28). Fancy, Jesus giving rest as a pillow! As head to pillow, place the problem on Jesus Christ!

Jesus suffered that you might rest in that suffering

When John Paton the Missionary to Samoa wanted a word in the native language which would describe "rest" he called in a native, sat down on a chair and asked what the word was in the Samoan language. He then took his feet off the floor and leaned all his weight on the chair. He asked again for the native word that described leaning all your weight on it. This word was included in his translation to describe the word "rest" in the New Testament.

His rest is free! It is sure! It is the rest of the permanent fixture! It is a rest from the past in a new future. It is large, wholesome and it puts back in what the world has taken out. Rest, as the Scottish salmon which struggles up stream until it comes to peaceful waters and there it rests in peace. Rest in Him as the water rests in the vessel. Rest, where the storm is calmed. The place where agitation ceases. Rest, where it is Heaven, where peace is on the throne and all swords are beaten into ploughshares. Rest in the heart of God where all things are brought together for good in the control of Jesus Christ. Some things will give you rest in a measure. They will proclaim — Come and rest a while. Jesus gives rest all the while from the wiles of the devil. All the time we are trusting Him and in His love, rest, even as the water beetle with a great bubble around it, and inside another world, another atmosphere. My tears are your tears, Your rejection is My rejection, Your ill treatment is Mine. I am one with you under the black garment of sorrow. I am the other side, the other part, the Siamese twin. I am behind the drawn blind.

Jesus suffered real pain

In the New Testament signs were written all across lives, in and through every area which read: Keep out! Jesus will be prosecuted! Warning! Danger! There is deep darkness here, there is a cutting edge and a cliff edge, enter at your own peril! He knew darkness by the space of three hours (Mark 15:33). Rejected by men and by God He totally identifies and understands rejection. He tasted vinegar and gall on that Cross (Matthew 27:34). He knew sorrow and He knew peace. He had feelings, he had disappointments, rejections — "we are legion and we are many". These were more than thorns in a crown on His Head, these thorns were growing on branches and in human hearts, and He had to deal with them. Anything which moves the mind was in Christ Jesus. We have One Who understands and in understanding He undertakes for us. It was not only the objective emotions which He passed through, it was also the negative emotions such as doubt, fear, darkness, misunderstanding and shame. The Book of Hebrews states "He was heard in that He feared" (Hebrews 5:7). In darkness and under stress until He sweat great drops of blood (Luke 22:44). His sufferings are unknown in depth because He suffered as the One from heaven. We suffer as those who are of the earth.

When Isaiah 53:3 refers to Jesus as a Man of Sorrows he doesn't stop there. Jesus did not just taste cod liver oil, He drank the whole bottle. His was not just a measured suffering, it states that He carried our griefs and our sorrows. He laboured with a labour of love to take our sorrows. The packs and the burdens are tied to the back of the donkey. Samson lifting the gates of Gaza is but a poor illustration of Jesus, our burden-Bearer (Judges 16:3).

Rest the burden of suffering on Jesus

Years ago, in caves and archways where beasts of burden had to travel, and sometimes even in stables, small shelves were made so that the animal, whilst it was feeding, could rest its burden on them. There are many such shelves in Jesus Christ. There is one made for your burden. He was wounded, bruised, stricken and smitten, chastisement was upon Him, and by His stripes we are healed (Isaiah

53:5). In the lash and the mark of the whip cutting into His flesh a place is made for you to place your burden of life. He was bruised so that, at the end of it all, a Man could be there to understand what our pains are saying to God. He could be the Interpreter of the unknown tongue. The pain and the problem which have a language of their own could be interpreted by Christ. The battles of life are interpreted by the Victor. He is the Linguist of love. He is the opposite to Babel (confusion) in our suffering.

You can read stories, tell stories, see pictures of famous places, but the authority is stamped upon your conversation when you can say, "I have been there! Better still, I was born there!" Yet only Jesus can say, "I died there!". To all who ever suffered He is the Suffering Christ. To all who ever need love, He is the loving and the lovely Christ. To the lonely, He stands alone, no-one wanting to know Him. He came unto His own and they rejected Him. To those who rejoice, He rejoices with them in God. When the rain clouds gather and storms break, when the whip falls onto the naked flesh, wherever blood is shed causing great gaping wounds, He is there — Jehovah Shammah — the Lord is there! (Ezekiel 48:35).

Jesus is touched with the feelings of your infirmities

When we thirst, He thirsted. His dying words were, "I thirst" (John 19:28). When we are in need, He was in need. He performed no miracle for selfish reasons. He did not fill His own basket or larder with bread. The five thousand who had been so hungry were not fed for the sake of Jesus. That miracle was not performed to give Jesus a ready-made lunch. Jesus did not fill His own waterpot with wine. What He did, He did for others. When love went from Him it was that it might make a place in His heart for another. When there is cruelty, remember that so also was He treated. The Darling of God was placed into the den and into the mouth of the lion. Whatever form sickness takes, whatever the manifestation of symptom is, whichever way the mental health or nervous system goes, Jesus has been that way before. When they pressed cruel thorns into His head they must have seemed like hot pokers piercing His flesh, the fingers of hell poking into Him. The flames of torment burnt fiercely. The

God of the burning bush was not consumed. Jesus did not sink, He did not even have to swim for it, He trusted God through it all. That is why He is seated at the right hand of the Majesty on high. The work that He seeks to do is done by His other Self, the Holy Spirit — His Pope and Vicar on earth. He cries over every perplexity; He trumpets over disease and hurt: "It is finished!" (John 19:30). "Be of good cheer, I have overcome the world! The world I have created, I have now overcome. As a ship loosed from its moorings I have brought it back and made it secure" (John 16:33). The nails in His hands and feet, the sword in His side, the dropping of the Cross into the hole in the ground must have jolted the whole make up of Jesus Christ, yet not one thing came apart or drifted from its place. All His suffering did was to settle in His heart even more the purposes of God. It brought Him to the place of being pressed down, shaken together and running over. He suffered it manfully, gently and thoroughly for you and for me. He could have called a thousand angels, but instead He called up millions of reserves within Himself! His humanity wasn't simply passed on to Him — end of the matter, case dismissed. There were things He had to pass through so that, in passing through He could help others. He began as we did, in the womb, and went on to the tomb. Neither held Him back but simply took Him on and on. Peter in his Epistle says: "He has left footsteps for us to follow" (1 Peter 2:21) — markings in the granite of life.

Jesus is a brother in suffering adversity

In His conversations after the Resurrection Jesus is so understanding. The pity of God is seen in the God of all pity. As the two journeyed from Jerusalem to Emmaus they found a wealth of comment to help with their sorrows when Jesus drew near (Luke 24:15). His nearness always does. Nearness is newness. He opened their understanding as opening a book at the correct page, headed "Suffering and Understanding". They had an exegesis on Jesus. Jesus commenced as a stranger, but He stayed long enough to become their friend (Luke 24:18). Verse 25, Jesus deals with their folly and lack of faith. He deals with their doubts. He deals with their suppositions, bringing their minds into focus and letting them discover how the Divine Mind is at work behind the scenes all the time.

The women came to the tomb with spices and found sunshine, but there was a problem...a stone had to be rolled away. Who will roll the stone away for us? Where is the army? Where have the Roman soldiers gone? Just a couple of women and they could not move the stone, yet when they arrived at the tomb, it had been rolled away! (Mark 16:3, 4).

Jesus deals with the doubts suffering can produce

John 20:24...Jesus dealt with Thomas, as a Man of Sorrows. There are many who believe that Thomas was not simply a twin but that he had a twin nature within him, a part clinging to one thing and a part which clings to another. We also have a part of us which is strong and brave and a part which gives in easily. Sometimes we stand with Peter as a rock, then we fly with him as Simon, son of Jonas the dove. The rock nature and the dove nature seem part of us all. We want to believe yet we are so easily deceived. Jesus dealt with every doubt of Thomas as the Son of Man but also as the Man of Sorrows. The first thing Jesus does in John 20:27 is to bring irrefutable evidence to the fingertips of Thomas. Thomas buried all his fear, all his foibles, all his human fumblings into the holes in the hands of Jesus Christ. As he reached out and touched Him there was an acknowledgement that Jesus had heard every word, even though He was absent when the words were spoken. As absent from Thomas when Thomas spoke, as Thomas was when Jesus appeared. God does not deal with us as metal or tin. He does not apply a tin opener. God deals with us in feelings because feelings are part of us. That is why Jesus had to be a Man of Sorrows. A servant, yes. A Saviour, yes. A Shepherd, yes...but more importantly, a Man of Sorrows. He became the Man of...you can supply the other word.

Sorrow can take as many forms as the colours in an autumn leaf. It can be in the death of a loved one; a misunderstanding; a quarrel: that which did not work out: sickness. If it is the death of a loved one, be assured that Jesus comes to the funeral as the Rose of Sharon. He stands as the Lily of the Valley, the unseen and sometimes unheard of Mourner. God is One with His people in death. We don't send out invitations to a funeral, and we don't have to invite God into our thorn bush before He comes. "Before you call, i.e. right early, before the dawn, I will answer you" (Isaiah 65:24).

Isaiah 29:2...The word "sorrow" is lamentation. There is a Book of Lamentations written by Jeremiah. God brings him through it all.

Jesus was smitten with your suffering

Deuteronomy 28:65...*Sorrow* is grief. Many times in the Books of Samuel and Job and in the Psalms it is a pang or a cord which so limits us. Genesis 42:38 it is *affliction*. In the Book of Ecclesiastes sorrow means *sadness* (Ecclesiastes 7:3). It would in that book! Job 3:10, it is labour. In the New Testament the word sorrow many times means grief, sadness, affliction, pain, torture and doubt. They are built up as walls, but the walls of Jericho fell down (Joshua 6:20). These sorrows are like small pieces of chaffing grit, but through a process grit is turned into a pink and blue mottled egg from which arises a beautiful bird of paradise. He arises from the dead and rolls not only the stone away but all stones which would shut out the light of His love, His care and His ministry. To those who sit in the shadow of death a great light has sprung up. Walls may be built around us but listen, He looses the prisoners! *He that follows me shall not walk around in darkness* (John 8:12). He is the Light at the end of the tunnel. He is the Light before you go into the tunnel and He is the Light which is switched on inside the tunnel! The darkest hour is before the dawn. So many times during the suffering and through the darkness we appreciate the light. When a cloud over-shadowed Jesus a voice came from it: *This is My Son* (Matthew 17:5; Luke 9:35). It is in that darkness, that pressure, that the black piece of coal becomes the diamond. There, in the dark, it receives all its lights and when it has been unearthed it needs the lapidary to cut and polish it in its own dust so that its brilliance may be seen by all. Thus it brings glory to the wearer and to the watcher. If the man who grinds it should make a mistake it will be shattered forever — as common as glass. Jesus makes no mistakes. The ways of God are more sure than the old landmarks. If God be for us He is more than all that are against us (Romans 8:31). He can triumph in such unusual ways and by such unusual methods. God's methods are manifold in variety. He never rubber-stamps anything. Look at nature and see eloquent testimony to this. He is your Man of Sorrows...your sorrows met in a Man.

Earthly men can prescribe without intimate knowledge, but not God. He does it all through Jesus Christ, our representative Man. Your government is on His shoulders.

A Man of Sorrows: maturity in sorrow as an example, and as an ensample[2] (1 Corinthians 10:11). In Him God's mercies combine to heal the hurt. Suffering can be a cord which ties and binds, but Jesus can turn it into a cord of love, such as lovers would wear around their necks near to their hearts. Suffering is that which can limit and lead to frustration if God is left out of it. Include the Man of Sorrows and you have found the code to the Hieroglyphics.

The voice of Jesus calms suffering

When Mary was at the tomb crying, it was the call and voice of Jesus which, with its urgency, brought her to the acceptance of Jesus not just as *Rab*, a man who came and did a day's work for you (John 20:16). She did not answer to that call with the normal word of *Rabbi*, meaning simply a teacher, one who had scholars listening to his teachings and interpretation of the Law. It was the word *Rabboni*, the word used for a great Master, the most excellent of His day. The *Don* of the Universities. The one who suggested what the words meant, who had people readily accepting their interpretations and built all their teaching on what He said. He was a foundation stone. He was the One Who set the rules. Disputes were settled by Him. One word from Him and arguments ceased as if no word had ever been spoken in anger. He decided what doctrine should be, just as Hillel or Gamaliel at whose feet the Apostle Paul listened. This Man of Sorrows was manliness enveloped by sorrows, but not engulfed by it. He was sent to help the lame, raise the dead, lift the burden with enough strength and to spare. Jesus had a heart for all and a strength for all to rely and lean upon. If one lower down the order, named Peter, did see those healed by his mere shadow, how much more could and would Christ heal and help? What strength there must be in the substance of the Master!

Looking to Jesus sustains us in suffering

I heard the story of the man who was badly injured in World War II. There was no anaesthetic to deaden the pain during an operation on his wounds. The only building they could use for the operation was a Church and the only table large enough was the altar at the front of the Church. When the wounded soldier was told of the situation he replied: "Turn me, so that from the altar as I am being operated on, I can see Christ on the Cross. If I am facing the Crucifix and can see the Face of Christ, I shall be able to bear the pain". As he looked on the suffering form of Jesus Christ he was able to undergo the operation. To look on Him is strength; to gaze on His suffering helps us. No cuts, no wound could ever match those of Jesus. It is the conscious presence of Christ which helps us through wounds and wars. It strengthens the faith just to see the Face. It turns pain into that acceptable part of life, given to all and received by all, some with strength, others with inability to cope. Jesus is Paradise opened and hell closed. It silences gnawing pain just to know that God knows. To assimilate the presence of Jesus is great strength. God's Son has laid in a manger of pain.

In Jesus we have a Jason. We all need a Jason in our lives, particularly when we face sickness and disease. Romans 16:21 — he is mentioned as one of the early Disciples in the Church. Paul sends greetings to Jason. The Apostle remembers him because his ministry is needed so much. It was mentioned by their leader. There were certain qualities in Jason — maturity needed by all — strength when called upon to suffer. Jason means *healing* or *he that cares*. Reflected in this believer at Rome is all that Jesus Christ is and all He can be made to us...wisdom, righteousness, sanctification and redemption, but also strength to bear as well as faith to believe. Those qualities in Jesus are the very aspects needed to help us to win through. Having done all, to stand.

NOTES

1. Dr. William Barclay, theologian, teacher, writer and lecturer in New Testament language and literature at the University of Glasgow. Quotation from *The Plain Man Looks at the Apostles Creed*, William Barclay, p.93.

2. Ensample — a type or a figure; the savour of the real.

5

The Grace and Glory of Suffering

There will be times when you require the grace of God. Times, even when your clock has stopped ticking. The days when burdens are as many as clouds. Days when worries are piled as high as dishes in a sink. God is there to help in every time of need. This chapter takes you into different lives, and you can see the grace of God flowing in from every angle. Our God is a very present help in trouble. He is more present than the trouble. That grace comes, and flows through young and old. It has no stopping place. It is never dried up or used up.

All the help we need is poured through the hand of the crucified Christ whom we saw as a Suffering Servant in the previous chapter. Each particle of grace is touched with His feelings for us. Jesus is the measure and measurement of grace. He always knows where to place it. He knew to put fish in water, and fruit on tree branches for accessibility. Be thankful that he knew to put hands on the end of arms, and feet on the end of your legs. What an awful mess we might have been in if God didn't know. He takes your need, and uses it as a door of opportunity, and through that door floods His grace.

Grace is when God steps in. It is when others have walked all over us, and God begins to walk with us. It can be the pouring in of the oil and the wine in healing virtue.

❉   ❉   ❉

The Grace of God, that which we do not merit but which we can inherit in Jesus Christ is measured according to the need. If that need is a circle, then it is circular; if it is a square, then it is squared; if oblong or rectangular, so is the grace. If the shape or the need be odd then grace is able to meet all within its own powers of capability. It is that which we desire and require which will stretch around the

75

need whatever that need may be. When we come to a bend or a spiral we need that which is before and that which is after, that which curves with the bend. There are moments in life when we need God to make all our beds in sickness. We need more than sheets, more than doctors, more than all that the Welfare State is able to offer. It is a need of the heart that sounds out in our own spirits as loud as any Church bell or alarm clock. There is a need to know that God is there, informing us, confiding in us and confirming to us that He cares. Through our pain God is sometimes shouting to us, but never at us.

Great grace means God makes us equal to the temptation

The Lord opens His hand and satisfies the desire of every living thing (Psalm 145:16). I need that hand which is flat and open to be turned over and sometimes to become an umbrella, when I am underneath it, protected by God and all His amazing grace. I need God to become my Protector of the Faith. To know that God is with us can be the source of greatest strength. It can mean the lengthening of patience and the deepening of love. In that which I cannot, do not, dare not understand, I need to see and to know His hand at work. I need to know in sickness and in health that I am still part of God's handiwork despite the fact that I am weary, worn and sad. In my spirit I am like the blind eye which cannot see and the stiff leg which cannot walk. Disease is more than that which is physical. The physical limits the spiritual. I feel that this body is a cage and, because of all it is called upon to suffer, it needs a singing canary placing within it. Only the grace of God can do that for me. He can. He cares. He will. He is willing. He must. He has promised never to leave me nor forsake me. He is the Master of all — He is altogether Master of all situations, including mine. There are no sleeping, waking, walking or sitting moments when God is absent. When pain comes in, then God becomes my comfort. God steps in not with something I feel but through my knowledge of Him, the conviction of faith standing as a guard outside Buckingham Palace, garrisoning my heart with peace. God may have been preparing you for this moment for a long time. Thirty three years led Jesus to Gethsemane and the Cross. It is the knowledge of faith, the certainty of trust, the strength of leaning. It works for the homeless, the downcast, the depressed. Help means time of need. Time of need added to help brings us to the equation of grace. Grace equals need met. In sickness and in health we need the grace of God...grace for race, for place, for pace and grace for grace. It is out of His fulness that we receive it, though it be *manifold* — many coloured and folded over like a blanket waiting to be turned back to cover me fully (John 1:16; 1 Peter 4:10). As the blankets on the bed are turned back, I discover the grace of God even between the sheets and sharing my bed of sickness. I rest in grace. I sleep, eat, live and breathe the grace of God. He gives me so much grace I wonder that He has any left for others! I have a great need for grace, but I have a great grace for my need! My need was great but not greater than grace in all its glory.

Grace appears in the form of many helps. Grace has many aspects and many hands which make light work of that which has become so heavy. Sickness can be a discovery in recovery. What I am, my condition, whether strong and brave or weak and faltering reveals the depths at work in others. The place we are in is as a stage and we are actors, each performing that which contributes to the whole. Sometimes it is not a stage at all but a black out of the way place. It is a bed of sickness, a thorny branch or nettle which I have been called upon to grasp fully. It makes me gasp fully! It is that which is surrounded by worry and fretting, a tunnel with no light at the end of it. In these adverse situations we need help with that which surrounds us.

Grace to a child is so soothing

Simon[1] is an insurance executive, young, big, strong, with hair like a raven. He was built to last, like a bridge! Julie, his wife, is a trained nurse, young, strong, vivacious and humorous with an inward strength which would challenge any Samson. Their second child, a daughter, was losing weight and they could not understand the reasons for this. They prayed about it, but there was no change. The child, Katie, was an avid syrup drinker, almost, at two and a half years of age, an addict to sweet juices! She loved to have her little bottle filled time and time again with sweet drinks. Life for the child was a bottle with sweet juices in it. The parents took the child to the paediatric nurse, who proceeded to examine her in every way, after which they were told that the child's healing depended on the most dramatic and drastic measures — she would have to give up the drink! The syrup, I mean! Well, the parents were worried — how would they break the news to Katie? What would she do? How would she respond? When little Katie went to bed that night, Daddy said: "Katie, you cannot have any more of that drink from the bottle, it is making you poorly". It was the worst news the child had ever received — worse than a bar of chocolate being snatched from her. She would not sleep. "The only thing I can do for you is to pray", said Daddy, so he asked Jesus to help Katie get to sleep. She went to sleep. In the night she awoke, wanting her bottle, and again Daddy said, "I can only pray". This he did, and she again went to sleep. The following night — how would it all work out? The little girl did not ask for the bottle with juice in it, but said, "Daddy, pray!" This he did and she went soundly to sleep, and slept all through the night. Ever since that time whenever Katie goes to bed or awakes in the night, the first thing the child at nearly three years of age says, is, "Pray, pray"...and she then sweetly and wonderfully goes to sleep. Just like the ship in the storm when Jesus said, "Peace, be still!". The Mother, with a gleam in her eye, tells all her baby sitters that the best soother is a word of prayer! Julie and Simon and their daughter Katie found grace to help in time of need.

Grace, the unfathomable riches of His grace

Jim and Jane were both out of work. Previously they had had good jobs with good salaries, but now they were left with just the Government allowance, or dole. How would they manage? A growing family, big, strong, hungry and developing all the time. They required large meals...in fact, if Daniel had been placed with them Jane wasn't too sure that he wouldn't have been eaten, they had such voracious appetites! The biscuit tin was always empty, sweets never lasted long, food disappeared from plates as quickly as it was put on them. Then, there was the commitment to their Church. They loved the little Church and its Pastor, but, out of work, how could they give to support the man who ministered to them? Should they remove their finances? Would they still be expected to give in these hard times? God knew their pockets had holes in and everything slipped through. Jane was of a strong nature and she decided they would honour God with their substance first and then trust Him that He would meet their needs. There were doors and windows in Heaven, and God was in control. This they did. Some folks thought that starvation would become another member of this little family. The children went to play in the attic — a place they had not been allowed in too much, a sort of "regions beyond". Suddenly there was such a shout and the Mother thought that one of them had fallen, yet it wasn't the shout of someone who was hurt, it was the shout of a prize winner, mingled with delight. She hurried to the scene and gazed in wonderment at her children. In their games they had come across a tin box and it was full of old money, pressed down, shaken together and running over! Aladdin's cave! An old bank which had been hidden and closed in the past. It was the place where the Almighty keeps His reserves for a rainy day. It was pouring, but with money not rain. It was the miser's money box! They had struck gold — or, rather, gold had struck them. They, too, found grace to help in time of need. They proved that in the extremes of poverty we have an extremely rich God. The riches of His grace were revealed in earth's riches, coin and king shaped.

The nature of His grace

Miracles of healing and needs met just at the right time do happen. Not all are called to suffer, some are healed in many different ways, as we shall discover in the final Chapter of this book. A way of escape provided in difficult circumstances through faith in a living God. The stories are more abundant than bees in a hive and time and space will not allow complete revelation at this time. In Eternity there will be some great testimony telling triumphs, all the triumphs of grace. It is there, where all will be shown in substance as the rainbow coloured workings of God — no wonder we shall worship! All the testimonies of how God met needs and lifted spirits will be joined together to make one huge myriad miracle. We shall all contribute to singing a new song and, because of grace, will join together forming a new race, saying: "You are worthy of honour, praise, glory, majesty and dominion". The glory of needs met and testimony given will be in Emmanuel's land.

Grace is that which bestows occasions of pleasurable delight. It is when the needy and the hungry are filled with good things. It is the word which was used by the Greeks to describe a statue, perfect in form, requiring nothing, a term of beauty. That which restores beauty to life is grace. A thing well fitting is gracious. All that God allows is Heaven allowed. It is the best possible design for you. It was comely in shape and all parts added to the fulness. Every blow to the marble, every slight touch mattered because of what was going to be produced. It can describe beautiful speech such as a silver tongued orator could deliver, or poetic writings which are perfect in verse. This is what grace is seeking to work into us. Grace was a form of greeting when meeting — Acts 15 : 23. We should be wishers of grace upon the lives of others, that which will beautify the meek, that quality which makes the weak strong and true.

2 John 10:11, R.S.V. *"Greeting." King James Version, "God speed."* Praying and saying grace into grey graceless situations. When we say "God bless you" we are really saying, "God be with you". Grace is being placed at the disposal of another. Make grace your goal and you will surely score and be part of a winning team!

Grace to help in the time of need

Hebrews 4:16. *Find grace to help in time of need.*

Hosea 13:9. *But in Me is your help.* God is a very present help in the time of trouble. His power is stronger than trouble. His Presence is wider, deeper, higher than the trouble. He is able to trouble trouble! He is there when the trouble comes and when it leaves. Trouble is given in many words in the Bible. It can mean stress, trembling, burden, pressure, labour, toil, affliction, to be disturbed and vexed. Ezekiel 32:2, 13, it means to make muddy. These are the tokens of life. Grace which comes from God is as a sun and a shield in the time of trouble and deals with every type of trouble. God does not say *Trouble Me not, the door is shut!* (Luke 11:7).

A man was being interviewed for a position with Manchester City Council. They asked questions about the *Rest Factor*. "What would you do if you came under real pressure?" The Christian replied in such a way that it pulled the carpet right from under their feet..."I would just lean back and praise the Lord, uttering a quiet prayer which would be returned to my own soul as the answer and it would quieten my own spirit". Grace to help in time of need.

Maturity requires grace

George was eighty-six years of age. He didn't know conversion until he was well into his seventies, but when he came to Christ it was real and deep. At eighty-six he had what is commonly known as a stroke. Would it be the end? He began to fight back and having recovered to some degree he agreed to go to the local Day Care Centre. The people there immediately knew that he was different. As they gathered round a table, each person was asked to do something which told about their lives, and George said that he would sing. Having been a church choir member and a member of a local male voice choir he felt he could accomplish something. He sang to them the lovely words:

"Because He lives, I can face tomorrow; because He lives, all fear
  is gone;
Because I know, I know Who holds the future, and life is worth
  the living, just because He lives."

Grace in the trial of your faith

John had just been told the worst possible news. They would have been better flaying him with a whip or swinging a sledge hammer at his chin — even that would have had a lesser impact than this news. They had confirmed that he had cancer! He walked through the hospital corridors and felt more lonely than Adam when he was the only man on the earth. All the "gut" feelings he had when he first heard the diagnosis were with him, he felt sick. His friends were far removed. It was just him and the disease. Was he alone? Didn't he trust the God he had trusted in for so many years? When the water comes to the bridge it must flow round it or under it. John realised the fulness of his Christian faith at that moment. Breathing deeply and drawing himself up to his full six foot, he strode on, trusting that the grace of God would turn bad news into something good. Had he not read in the Bible "that which was midnight blackness to Egypt became as the light of day to the children of God"? (Exodus 10:22, 23) As he pondered on these things it was as if a light had been switched on, illuminating every step of his way. That is a true happening. It took place some twenty years ago. John lived on by various means and he found the grace he needed. He lived to see his young family raised and to see happiness spread abroad because of his testimony to the grace of God in a difficult situation. He is still alive and well and is very active in his local Church.

✻   ✻   ✻

"Get that seen to!" — these were the words of a nurse to her father. He had a growth on his neck. "Dad, it has a head and it has roots, you need some medical attention!" The father, a believing Christian, prayed about the problem and booked an appointment to see his doctor. After prayer and the laying on of hands about a week before his actual appointment, the growth miraculously fell off his neck! He appeared before the doctor rather embarrassed. The doctor's diagnosis? "Well, I don't think you will need to see us again". During the time when the growth was on his neck, he needed grace to help in time of need, and it was supplied!

Healing grace to help

Not all are healed. Some are called to go through the thorns, like Paul, by life and by death that Christ might be magnified in the body. Some are called to walk along the blade of the surgeon's knife, others never approach the scalpel, yet all are called into grace and to undergo the operations of grace. To those who question the reasons why, Scripture then must ever be the arbiter. Has not the potter power over the clay to make one vessel unto honour and another unto dishonour? In the house of a great man there are many vessels and God is seeking that all might be of use, sanctified and fit for the Master's use.

* * *

Robert had never entered any hospital or had a day's illness in twenty-five years. Then he suffered six heart attacks. During one of them, drifting from consciousness into a state of unconsciousness, between Heaven and Earth, hovering between this world and the next, his wife had been more than a little alarmed. What would she do if he were to die? During his more lucid moments Robert was able to reassure her that it was "far better" to be with Christ (Philippians 1:21, 23).

> "This suffering has brought another dimension into my Christian experience. It has been made more open at both ends and has developed compassion in me which my Christianity never knew. It has stretched me rather than pulled me. It has made me stand up, rather than bowled me over. I feel a better person for it and God has put something into me which I have been able to pass on to others."

Grace to help in time of need.

The words "in time of need" — Hebrews 4:16, according to G.C. Morgan[2], could be translated "in the nick of time". Just at the right moment, when it is needed the most. Somewhere between the slip and the fall, God steps in. Sometimes he allows us to touch the depths of the earth in order that we might reach the heights of His Heaven. Acts 20:9, 10, we are allowed to fall, to hit the ground, then the Lord reaches to revive us. Sometimes He catches us as we are falling. God meets us at our point of need. Where pain strikes, when the burden is at its heaviest, when shoulders are bowed to the ground, that is where Grace comes in. Like water it will find its own level and as heat it will rise. As the flower seeks more light from the sun, so God turns us more and more towards Himself.

God's grace is at work before, through, and after the event

God grew the tree before Zaccheus was born, so that it might be there just when it was needed. It was of the right stature, with branches low enough for a little man, with a trunk wide enough to grip, and marks to help scale it. It was in the right place, just outside Jericho, where Jesus would pass by (Luke 19:5). Was there not a man who fell among thieves also in this same area? Oil and wine was poured into his wounds by the Good Samaritan (Luke 10:34).

Rev Chad Varah, the man who conceived and introduced the concept of the modern Samaritans, tells how they needed to have a certain telephone number which would spell "samaritan" on the old system. Each number corresponded with the relevant letter of the alphabet, as found on the old telephone dial, which spelled out the name "Samaritan". When they found the telephone under all the rubble in the house they had purchased to commence their work, the very number which they needed to spell the name so that everyone could remember it, was the very number of that telephone, yet they had had no prior knowledge of it. Chad Varah was convinced that God had put His stamp of grace on their endeavours. Time has proved that, for grace has poured through the work of the Samaritans like a river. They have certainly been a help in times of need. How many lives have been brought back from the brink and into the sunshine, only God Himself knows.

God so prospered the Prodigal's father that he could afford bread enough and to spare. God saw to it that there was a fatted calf and musical instruments in plenty — all the right ingredients in the right place for the homecoming of the son. God was working it out even as the son was feeding amongst the swine. In place of grunts — God gave grace! (Luke 15:17, 23).

Many times Oliver Cromwell would say to his soldiers: "God will help us in the nick of time".

To the thirsty God does not send water through a pipe — it runs freely as a river. He gives to us again and again. When we stop asking God does not stop giving. It is an essential part of the nature of God to give — more sky than we can gaze at, more stars than we can count, more flowers than we can smell, more water than we can drink. More, much more, God is all things to all men. He is the God of the seasons, the hours, the days and the minutes.

Grace means all things to all God's people

Harrods of Knightsbridge is so well known that, if you were to send a telegram addressed: "To All Things of London", it would be delivered to them! They became known as "All Things". The store had such a capacity for holding everything you wanted, and if it was not in stock they would arrange for it to be ordered. God is all things to help us in adverse circumstances. When we cannot see round the corner — God is already there. When we cannot see beyond the horizon, God shows us the setting sun.

In Genesis 33:1, Jacob is going out to meet his brother Esau after an absence of many years. In Genesis 33:9, as they meet, Esau says: "I have enough". An abundance — barns and pots which overflow. Jacob, who has been in contact with God, in Genesis 33:11, says: "I have enough". The word he uses is different. In Genesis 33:11 the word *enough* means *all*. I have everything. There is such a completeness in Christ. God is our help — Hosea 13:9, the word help is that same word in Genesis 2:18 - 20, where it describes the wife of Adam who was to be a helpmeet, one by his side, another ministry, another worker. Mark 16:20, God "working" with them and confirming the Word with signs following. God, as their "attendant", their "labourer"...that which John Mark was to Paul and Silas in Acts 13:5. They had him as their minister, under rower, one who helped out when the seas became rough and choppy. God is wanting to go with us and build with us. What shall we build together? Certainly not a division but something that will enhance our character until it is proclaimed of us:

"The King's daughter is all glorious within; her clothing is of wrought gold". (Psalm 45:13)

There are kingly qualities in grace

As the young child fell from the upper window it was heard to cry, "Okay God, now here's Your chance!". The child struck the ground and, to the amazement of all, was found with just a few bruises and scratches.

Your circumstances can become the Throne of God from which He administers His goodness. His love surrounds you, for every happening is God's way of dealing with your soul. He is waiting to illuminate your life into the fulness of the Light of the World.

As a handkerchief fell to the ground and was stained, the great artist simply drew around the stain and turned it into a beautiful flower, making the ugly stain the actual centre. This is what God does as we accept Him and find grace to help in time of need.

1 Samuel 14:49 — Malchishua, meaning The King of Help. Kingly, crowned, crises with Christ is better than a life of no trouble but without God. You have known Him as the King of Creation, Salvation, even Adoration, but what about "Help"?

"Got any rivers you think are uncrossable?
Got any rivers you can't tunnel through?"

These words were spoken by an American Construction Company who specialised in things thought impossible. The only thing impossible about anything is nothing!

Let the help of God form the shape of the need and you will find that there is a whole area of grace which is sufficient. Grace which can get under the need and lift it. Romans 8:26 describes the help of the Holy Spirit — He takes hold of one end and I take hold of the other. We need God to turn those crises in our lives into calm waters which allow us to steady the boat and put it back on course.

Even in instantaneous healing, a person needs grace to help at the actual point of healing, even as it was needed in the time of their need.

Grace poured through the Resurrection

Lindsay has two lovely daughters, they are the light of her pleasant life. Saying and doing those things which thrill the heart, and, sometimes almost making it miss a beat. It was time to talk to them both about the Death and Resurrection of Jesus Christ. As only a mother could, she proceeded (with dad absent at work) to tell them both about it all. There in their front room, on the lounge, with bent knees as the pulpit, mother began to expound the theology of her own heart about the death and resurrection of Jesus Christ.

As she continued, both their eyes opened wide with amazement when the resurrection of Jesus was mentioned, and it left a lasting impression on both their young hearts. There was a certain glow about their uplifted faces and kicking feet, as they sat listening enthralled as Jesus was enthroned. As far as Lindsay was concerned, here was unclaimed territory and unchartered waters, where the teachings of God and the throne of Christ must be established. Step by step they were led through one or two miracles, right to the cross and the cruelty shown to Christ. A certain stillness and quietness seemed to surround them. As they listened, at the feet of their Gamaliel, they could hear the voice of Jesus, and almost feel the pain as the nails entered his hands and feet. There was a childish gasp as the sword was pushed into His side, and the blood ran from it.

Gospel preached and word told, the children went quiet, and then they moved off to play. Just then the door opened, and in came tall daddy, smiling and looking at his children with such deep love. The children drew alongside their father, wanting to talk but not to listen. Lindsay began to explain how the children had been catechised. "I have told them how Jesus suffered on that cross, and how he died to forgive us our sins, and how He was buried. How they rolled a stone over the mouth of the cave in which they had placed him." Before she could utter another word, the three-year-old, Katie, said, "Mummy, mummy, tell him how he arose from the dead! Daddy, Jesus isn't dead, they didn't kill Him. He is still alive." There was silence as a beam of sheer delight spread over every face as they heard such good news. The little one had heard and retained an important truth. Here was grace to help in the time of need.

Pentecostal grace in other languages

Sarah had tummy ache. She belonged to a family who loved the Lord Jesus Christ, and believed in praying before they did anything else, even for those who were sick. Often in the church, and in the home, the sick would be prayed for. The more remarkable thing was, mother was a trained nurse, but not trained to the point where she ceased to ask God first. Common sense had taught them that if the prayer wasn't answered, and didn't seem to work, then they should see a doctor. This was even more emphasised because mum was a fully trained and qualified nurse, working in a local hospice. Suddenly the little girl, aged seven, appeared at the bottom of the stairs, "Mummy, will you pray for me. I have pains in my stomach. Immediately mum placed her hands gently as a bonnet on the little girl's head, and immediately she began to shake, and then cry. "Mummy, why am I crying?" she asked. "I feel so hot, and I am burning. What is happening?" Lindsay began to explain to Sarah, "when the Holy Spirit anoints us, we begin to cry because Jesus loves us so much. The Holy Spirit is as a fire, and that makes us feel really hot. In Acts, chapter 2, tongues of fire came upon the heads of the disciples as they received the Holy Spirit." The daughter seemed satisfied with the answer, and said, "Well, I am so hot, I want to go back to bed." "Alright," said mum, as she led the way back to the bedroom, and settled the little one into the bed for the night. There was such a warm glow in the bedroom. Ten minutes later, there was a shout from the bedroom, "Quickly, mummy, come and pray for me! I want to love Jesus more and more. Lindsay placed her hand again on the child's head, and suddenly she began to speak in other tongues as the Spirit gave her utterance. "Sahmma dada, rartasferea, madareankin. .... lada mephareana..." and on she went. A little later she became quiet, placed her head on the pillow and went soundly to sleep. Next morning at about 7 a.m. Sarah, aged seven, suddenly ran from her own bedroom speaking in another language by the Spirit of God. She went straight into her mother's bedroom, jumped into bed, still speaking in this foreign language, and nestled in at the side of her mother still magnifying God in this New Tongue. Here was grace to help in the time of need for a little girl. Having an experience which she would never forget through time and into eternity.

Unprepared for universal and unexpected grace

Margaret's mum, Bessie, was 81 years of age. She had been a little dispirited. Dad was in hospital seriously ill. (All these stories are authentic, and can be validated.) It was a great burden to her, and she needed the grace of God to help her. That something extra was required at a time like this. Because of her commitments to hospital visits, there had been no time to go to the local church, which she loved so very much. Her daughter and son-in-law had come to see her, but before they left, they always prayed for her. This time it was going to be different. Both daughter and son-in-law were of a Pentecostal nature, and were convinced what the Scriptures have to say about the Holy Spirit, and the Gifts of the Holy Spirit. They believed that if one received the Holy Spirit, there would be some visible evidence, such as speaking in other tongues. Mrs Warwick had spent much of her Christian life seeking and asking God to fill her with the Holy Spirit, just like the disciples were filled. (See Acts 2:4, Mark 16:17.) She argued, if the God of the Acts of the Apostles was the same God today, then what happened then should happen now. For years she had been asking God to fill her with the Holy Spirit. To her the dispensation of grace was from the cross, stretching right into heaven, including the Last Days. Upon my sons and daughters I will pour out of my Spirit in the Last Days. Daughter and son-in-law laid hands on her, praying that she would receive the Holy Spirit. They believed that as they did, that the Holy Spirit would come and fill this waiting temple. They weren't quite ready for what did happen that day. God had plans they had never thought of.

Mother stood in her own front lounge with her hands stretched up to heaven, and asking God to fill her with His Spirit. Quite suddenly something happened. Those around were expecting her to speak with other tongues. Suddenly with a heavenly voice she began to sing in other tongues, in another language never learned, "Sha..ma.ra dee.libba, deeandee..mada berranti", and on and on she sang, rising higher, and then lower as she sang, with a pause between each word, as if waiting to receive the next word or line of the composition from heaven. Each line and each word was given a particular emphasis by a short hesitation in the singing. Did Paul and Silas sing like this in the Philippian prison? (Acts 16:25.) Truly this was a

New Song in the tongues of men and of angels. Around the house she walked, not leaping, but walking and praising God as his praises were sang from a thankful heart. Here was grace to help in the time of need. Here was grace that spanned the generation gap between Grandmother and Great grand-daughter. One might have thought that at 81 years of age, her life was complete, she had served her purpose. Her usefulness was all used up. There was no more in God for her. Grace doesn't work like that. God saw the need and had a reason to fill with the Holy Spirit in spite of the age. The grace of God saw a future for this aged saint. The child, Sarah, was not counted as being too young or not mature enough. Grace did it all. Grace was there to help in the time of need.

NOTES

1. Real names have been altered.

2. Quote from *7,700 Illustrations*, Paul Lee Tan (Assurance Publishers, America), p.511. "Timely Help" — see Vine's *Expository Dictionary of Bible Words* (Thomas Nelson), p.301.

6

Receiving Strength through Suffering

G race has been received, and yet, we need even further strengthening. The steel must be placed into the fire, and then plunged into the liquid time and time again until it is hardened. When all seems in vain, it is God who brings strength without measure. At the point of our weakness, there is a certain power which comes from God alone on the throne. That which God sends breaks the power of pain through a Presence. There is a pain barrier, and, it is at this that we know the ability of God which is so utility. He adds his ability to the grace in the previous chapter, and it is grace to help in the 'time of need'.

God doesn't send rainbows to a sunny sky, He waits for the clouds to form, and the sky to darken. There is no provision of a covert from the storm where and when there is no storm. The haven is provided in his love for those who are battered. In being ready to sink for the third time, there is a breathing space provided. There is a place where no water comes.

God reveals his ability in a show of strength on our part. Not as some great display, not the trumpet or bells, but, sometimes in the quiet whisperings of assurance. In the still, small voice — the voice of quiet whisperings.

❊   ❊   ❊

God, in Christ, is able. He has the power to enable us to be able in all situations. He is abundantly able, above all that we can ask or think. Hebrews 2:18 identifies Jesus Christ with everyone who is tempted. As you are tempted, so is He. His dimensions are your dimensions. The depth there is in God! His power is your power. Jesus is the other half. He is the line drawn alongside your line and He stands and stays with you in the midst of outer blackness or inner disconsolation. Jesus Christ is the same always. He is capable of holding and handling all sides of the complexity of any crises. He is God and therefore He is able to stand in all four corners at once. He is able to surround that which surrounds us. For the fiercest fight He is the fiercest foe! In order to bear all things we have to believe all things, and in order to hope all things we have to believe all things. Bearing leads to hoping and hoping to enduring (1 Corinthians 13:7). "Through Christ I can do all things" (Philippians 4:13). Using His ability, His powers of accomplishment, His word, and His Name.

In times of great storms and deluges, watermarks are left on certain walls and it is from these that all other floods are marked and measured. All our suffering is measured by the Captain of our Salvation and finds its comparison in Christ. Whilst on the Cross and during His life on earth you will find that colour which matches exactly what Jesus passed through.

Strength comes to our weakness

In certain towns, villages and cities, memorials are erected, stone columns which state that some famous person had once lived or visited...*John Wesley came here*, reads one;   *Dorothy and William Wordsworth lived here, states a plaque on Dove Cottage. William Shakespeare performed here...Rudyard Kipling wrote some of his poems in this place*...yet how much greater when you know Jesus Lives Here! Jesus Christ is here. When He arose from the dead the angels said "He is not here, He is risen". That puts Him alongside every suffering saint. He is not dead and gone, but alive and working alongside us. Even ships will give a history of their captains and their voyages of the past. From the sufferings of Christ you will find a helping Hand, a welcoming Voice, and a radiant Smile. There is always sunshine in shadow. We are called only to suck the sweet, it is Jesus who drinks the vinegar. We are allowed to feel the warmth, it is Christ who goes through the fire, His soul is bared to the fiercest wrath of hell, in order that my soul might reach Heaven.

The text above the bed reads: "And it came to pass".

God is able to strengthen

I remember seeing a building firm which was simply called **ABLE**. *Builds walls well. We can erect extensions. Our work is to make bricks and mortar into homes. We turn wood and brick into houses that become homes. Our Popular built homes are very popular...* all this was written on the firm's letterhead — all good phrases, yet summed up in the one word **ABLE**. So also is Jesus Christ in rebuilding a life..."Believe ye that I am able to do this?" God performs many miracles as He restores that which has been snatched away. He is a God of might, of power, of capability and of ability. From the wrecks of life He brings prized possessions. As the Roman leaders would march up the Appian Way bringing their spoils of war, so also does God, but He marches up the Christian Way. Sometimes the erosion takes place slowly, imperceptibly until we discover too late that what was once so vibrant and healthy has gone, that simple, childlike trust has been lost. An enemy has done this. We are knocked down, but not knocked out! Bruised but not smashed, beaten but not bowed, blood stained but not dead! We are like the vine after the Husbandman has been to it and shown no mercy, the pruning hook and the knife have waged their war, there has been a cut and there the ripest, fullest and sweetest fruit will be seen. He knew there was a weakness which could neither bear fruit nor sustain it. It had to bleed so that the sap would travel freely into the branch.

The transforming strength of God

I know of a building firm named *Transformation*! We will change things! The next best thing to a new creation — we can make all the difference. We can erect what is in your mind. Your pleasure is our measure! Again, the one word describes it all — Transformation. All power is given unto Jesus Christ in Heaven and earth, to build on earth and to prepare in Heaven. It is far reaching power. It is real and is moulded into the shape of our need by grace. It fits everyone, no matter the shape or the size. There are no corners and there are no parts which are unreached or untouched. *Behold I make all things new* (Revelation 21:5). *Old things are passing away, all things are becoming new* (2 Corinthians 5:17).

2 Corinthians 6:2, Hebrews 2:18, the word which makes all the difference between weak and strong, lost and found, first and last, peace and perplexity, is the word *succour*. It explains the position of God. It is like a seed or a bulb waiting for a spring call into action, beauty and design. God was involved all the time and I knew it not. That faith which so imparts revelation to me was absent. I was saying, *Who is it?* "It is the Lord". He has taken a step back into the shadows. He has placed His nail pierced hands around the candle light to keep it from being extinguished. God alone can supply the constant flow of that which is needed. The Succouring God for the suffering man. He is a God Who does not change. *I am the Lord, I change not* (Malachi 3:6). It is not a matter of yesterday, today and tomorrow — God lives in the today and He acts in the Now! Such healing balm means that He cares, He cradles, He cuddles. He is there right by my side, and His very presence is proof of His caring. Care and love does not mean giving all the time or giving in to demands, it is a realisation that He knows best and His best is being worked out for me in the best possible way.

The strength required is not easily recognised or received

When Sir Winston Churchill was rejected by the electorate of Britain at the end of World War II, one man said, 'It is a blessing in disguise". Churchill replied, "It is well disguised, that is all I can say."

Christ is in every crisis. A crisis is His crusade. He is not nailed to a Cross but nailed to your heart and to your situation, as One Who is able to succour. Never have any doubts about the ability of God to take you up, around or through it all. When we come to the mountain, if we do not have the faith to remove it, then God will give the strength to either climb it or go round it. The scenery is much better from the top! He will make it come to pass. Eventually it will be as a faded image. Where there has been hurt, pain, sadness, there will be strength as we trust Him. "Through our God we shall do valiantly!" Prime Minister Gladstone had this text over his bed *You will keep him in perfect peace, whose mind is stayed on You* (Isaiah 26:3).

God succours through grace. He flows into lives and living and turns them into hope, peace and joy.

Matthew 3:9 — *"God is able to raise up children from these stones."* This heavy burden, this trial, can develop into something human and tender. Stones can be shaped but they cannot grow, retaining their hardness of character. Children are expressions of life and love and joy. As long as there are children on the earth there is hope for the nation. In every stone there is a child needing Jesus to say *"Arise! Talithi Cumi! Get up and go on!"* (Mark 5:41). Let that stone of suffering and that rock of offence become as the Chief Corner Stone. Let suffering find its way to the top of the stone and let succour give a helping hand, so that the very stone becomes an altar made without hands, to bear fire and sacrifice. You will win as Christ succours you. Conscious realisation of the presence of Jesus breaks rocks and brings forth children, the experiences which He gives. Sickness turns a crowd into friends, helpers, healers. Your heart, not your home, filled with trophies of His grace through His succouring of you.

Strength is multiplied and applied by grace

Can I misuse a Bible text? *"Great grace was upon them all"* (Acts 4:33). Grace comes on every problem, and within the area of sickness it is also the help to bear it or beat it. No sickness is the end. It may be an ending, but then, that suggests a beginning. We need something from God which, like cords of love, bind us closer to Him and renews our dedication and determination to go on. *"Go in this thy might, you mighty man of valour, the Lord is with you."*

One of the meanings of El-Shaddia is *"the many breasted God"* — the God Who is the source of all sustenance, the all sufficient God[1] (Genesis 28:3). It points to the excellence of His bounty, the fulness of the riches of God Who waits to share such with His children. If heirs, then joint heirs with Christ. God allows us to be placed in circumstances beyond our control that we might know His full control. Through weakness we discover His strength. Like Jonathan in 1 Samuel 14:27, we taste the honey from the "rock" and our eyes are enlightened. We have the light in our eyes as of a new day, our vigour is renewed and we are ready for battle. We have the strength to use the weapons of our warfare.

God gives us much attention as He succours us. He spends as much time on the fine detail as on the large points, giving to us His all. He is that super-abundance which we all need. During the feeding of the five thousand the bread which was broken, multiplied and passed from one to another would be fresh to each one, no two people had the same piece (Matthew 14:21). Grace is like that. When God succours us, He has a portion and the place of the apportioning shows how perfect His timing is. Everything in its time is beautiful. Read Ecclesiastes, Chapter 3.

Weakness requires new strength

Temptation is not only connected with sin, it is also a part of sickness. We are tempted, as Job's wife was, to receive and to give the advice of *"curse God and die"*. This is from the devil's manual of theology, it is not from the heart of God. Yet Job's spirit prompted him to reply *"Shall we not receive both good and evil from the Hand of God?"* If the words Lord and Sovereign Lord are to mean anything to us, it is that God is the Lord over every realm. Remember the words of Jesus *"All power is given unto Me in Heaven and in earth"* (Matthew 28:18). That power, be it in succouring or in sustaining, must be seen to work in you. In the Old Testament the Names of God are not revealed all at once, but little by little, and to different people. In differing situations God is revealed as the God for that time and place. In Psalm 23 the Names of God are all shown. At a time when Abraham was fearful, God said, "I am your shield" (Genesis 15:1). To Moses, God revealed Himself as "Jehovah", the covenant keeping God unto all generations. To Jacob, He is the God of thy fathers. To others He is the God of Abraham, Isaac and Jacob. Even as nature, in trees, sea, sky, bird, bush, rain, river is revealed, so in and to our natures is God revealed that the glory might be seen. It is the excellency of the power that is Godward, not manward. It is the discovery that there is treasure in earthen vessels. Life is a discovery and the best routes and greatest discoveries are made when God becomes the Topographist!

In sickness we are brought to a place of weakness, but out of that weakness must come strength. We can become a channel of peace. So often, because of grace, weakness and wilfulness have been turned into strength and mourning into joy. The problem has been used by God to stretch you, yet He allows His help to enter in at the most needy spot. Human beings apply medicine and plaster, will rub some aching back at the right place, the sorest point, and it is at that tender spot that God Himself shows His tenderness. He acts swiftly and gently and His bedside manner is all manner of good towards us.

We find the level places on the floor and there we again learn to stand. Sickness is sometimes meant to mature our faith. In Hebrews 11:37, they were *"sawn asunder"*, tempted...the evidence of things hoped for and the title deeds of things not seen had to be seen in their living and loving. Your severe trial can be as a constant wearing away because of the monotony of it all, as if we are being cut through — sawn asunder. It is no optical illusion, it is no imagery, it is real. Satan means to pull you down to hell. God means it to lift you up to Heaven. What was meant for evil to you, God has turned into good.

In the Book of Esther, Hamaan who was against the Jews was hanged on the very gallows devised for Esther, Mordecai and the Jewish nation (Esther 7:10).

Resting means strength for resisting

The idea of temptation is a piercing and you become as a dartboard. Satan expects more darkness to enter the soul through piercing and suffering, and that is when God allows ever more light to shine right in. Satan tears to pieces, whilst God pieces together. Satan intends destruction — God intends design. It is part of the *"all things working together for good"* (Romans 8:28), because you love God. It can take the form of discipline, as well as sickness. The thought in *"temptation"* (Matthew 6:13) may be that of the Assayer of Silver who sits by the furnace waiting for the dross to be removed in order that he can further refine the silver. He waits until he can see his image reflected in the metal and as the Refiner he knows at what temperature the dross and the precious metal will separate. The Lord knows that the fiery trials which come upon us can refine our faith, making it more precious than much gold. We refine gold, which ultimately will perish, yet God refines nature and builds up faith making it strong so that it will never perish. The key words used in Christ's messages to the Churches in the Book of Revelation are *"I know"* (Revelations 2:2, 9, 13, 19, 23). All that glitters is not gold, but all that which is gold has been through the fires of affliction. God is able to succour. He brings help. Helps are the frappings which were passed under a ship during a severe storm, ropes which were lashed underneath and which were carried on deck as reserves, ready to be used in emergencies. Some ropes held in various loose objects and would prevent them from being washed overboard. During a storm the main mast was likely to be torn from its moorings and the helps would sustain it during the wind and the rain.

In *Pilgrim's Progress*, the Christian allegory written by the Bedford tinker John Bunyan while in prison, Christian saw Help coming towards him, showing him the steps out of the Slough of Despond. When he was asked how he came to be in the Slough of Despond, Christian's reply was *"Fear followed me so hard that I fled the next way, and fell in"*. Help replied, "Give me thy hand", and taking hold of it, he set Christian on solid ground. Every circumstance that befalls us is to allow us to get to solid ground, the solid ground of redemption in Jesus. We travel from the marshy bog onto solid ground, and it is at that stage that you can then pull others out of their quagmires. From sinking sands we are lifted with tender hands until we dwell on higher plains.

We can be winners with God's strength

Sometimes we need to pray the old Negro spiritual *"Lord, stand by me!"*. God only stands on ground that is firm and sure. In Him there is no variableness or shadow of turning. He is all one.

The old London Society used to have men stationed near to ponds or lakes which had frozen and, if anyone fell in, their job was to fish them out. They were given the title of *"Helps"*. For those skating on thin ice, there is help available. Sometimes we take tumbles and fall even when engaged in pleasurable pursuits.

Jesus, because He too has been tempted, can meet you at your lowest point, at rock bottom you will find Jesus Christ. When the woman of Zarephath, the *"place of refining"* for Elijah, reached the bottom of the cruse of oil and the end of the flour barrel, God was there (1 Kings 17:9, 10). Zaccheus came down the tree and at the foot of the tree was Jesus Christ (Luke 19:5). You can never sink lower than the love of God. When all of life seems alarming, then Christ ensures that we come to no harm but brings reassurance that we must not fear him who can only limit or kill the body, but must have reverential fear for Him who can kill both soul and body.

In days gone by, when a train arrived in the station after travelling some distance, one man was appointed to go along with a hammer and bang the metal wheels to see how they sounded and from that sound he could tell whether or not there was a weakness in the wheels, whether they had somehow developed a flaw in travelling which could possibly de-rail the train. It was the blow of the hammer, not the whistle or the waving of a flag which discovered this. It didn't matter whether you were in first class or third class, or how much the journey had cost, your carriage wheels had the same treatment. The guard or station master had ears which were tuned to certain sounds, and they acted upon those sounds. If the train was found to be weak, then it was shunted into sidings for repair, and, after welding, shaping and tightening, it would be ready again to run straight and true. As a child I lived near to the railway sidings and have often seen the man with the pot of axle grease going from wagon to wagon, greasing the wheels. Each wheel had a square box with a lid, and he would thrust grease in on the end of a stick, thus keeping the wheels turning and the axles from overheating. Sometimes in life it would appear as if we are like those trains, but there is a succouring process taking place, a pattern and form, all of which are being created as we pass through the Valley of Baca (Psalm 84:6), leaving it as a place filled with pools of soft water, even as the waters of Shiloh. Refreshment is there, filled buckets for thirsty sheep, blessings for others. Horses, camels, donkeys, whole caravans are refreshed by what we leave behind. Jesus is our glorious example.

The strength of the Comforter

A promise to all who are in difficulty is given in John 16:7. The word *"Comforter"* in the *King James Version* and *"Counsellor"* in the N.I.V. is also *"Helper"* in the *Living Bible*. The whole idea behind the Helper is not that we might be consoled or just hugged, although that is part of it, but the word which we use for comfort is to *"come alongside"*, to surround us like a fort. It is to know that we have an armoury in the love of God. I once saw an old painting depicting the Battle of Hastings. The troops were all lined up ready for battle, but on closer inspection it was easy to see a certain amount of terror on their faces at having to face King Harold's troops. The King was behind his soldiers, sticking a spear into the backsides of some of them, to spur them on, and underneath the painting were the words: *"William comforteth his soldiers"*.

A strange use of the word *"succour"* is found in the New Testament. In Romans 16:2, it is the feminine of the word found in Hebrews 2:18. The word is *"Succourer"*, and means a protectress, a patroness. The motherly, womanly side of God, caring and cherishing as a nurse cares and cherishes. The word in Hebrews 2:18 was used by the people of Athens and it was a title. The person given the title had the position of seeing to the welfare of those who were resident aliens, who had no right of citizenship or civic rights. Our citizenship is in Heaven. Among the Jews the word meant wealthy patron, one who had many riches and could afford to look after others in sickness and in health. To succour is to give aid, to love and to lift, to help and to heal, to enquire and to enable. The English meaning is *"to run up to"*, as if running and holding a bottle of cordial at the same time. That is the eagerness, the willingness, the alacrity of God when coming to our aid. It is more than lucozade! Before you call, even before the echo sounds, I will help you? No! Before you call, I will answer you!

Recognise the source of your strength

Don't be like the man who, when the floods came, found himself stranded on an island and prayed, *"Lord, send help to succour me"*. The Police came to escort him to safety, but he replied *"No, I am not leaving here until God sends help"*. The Ambulance and Paramedics came offering help and a safe journey, but this too was refused on the grounds that he was waiting for God to send help. Along came the fire engine and crew, and as a last attempt they landed a helicopter, but the man, with flint-like determination refused all help saying *"I am waiting for the Lord to deliver me"*. He died. When he awoke in Heaven the first question on his lips was *"Lord, why didn't You answer my prayer and send help?"* The Lord replied, *"I did, the Policeman, the Fireman, the helicopter, but you did not recognise or accept the help I sent to you."*

We only see help and receive it when we look for it. God doesn't necessarily send help in the way we expect it to come sometimes.

God's strength is above, below and around us

The word which we use in the English language *"succinct"* means it is under girded, concise, terse, held in and to the point. It did not go round in circles and neither will God when He comes to help us in time of need. He will not hover as a vulture does, but will come in as a missile on target, homing in on that target.

From a position of great strength, Jesus Christ is able to succour us. He can turn away any wind, and can send the sun towards us in our state. Water can arise out of the ground when we are thirsty and in need. Paul said, *"Whatsoever state I am in, I have learned **therewith** to be content"* (Philippians 4:11). Paul was content with Christ in any dark situation, knowing that Christ is Light. To Paul, one state was as good as another. He realised that he had to learn in any state in any situation to be content, to learn to be self sufficient in Jesus Christ. He had to draw his sufficiency from an Eternal Foundation, from the Eternal nature of Jesus Christ. Contentment, because he was in Christ more than he was in that state, came to him as some poured out perfume, reminding him of the Rose. All the suffering and inconvenience did not matter, Paul had got to know succour and the Succourer.

There are things in Jesus Christ, healing, suffering, endurance, which are ours and all are a part of what is in the heart of God for us. Life in God is a discovery of that which has never happened to us before, we are Discoverers, discovering, uncovering, yielding, asking, taking, doing, learning. All are part of the process in Jesus Christ. "All things are yours."

> *"Whatsoever things are true, whatsoever things are honest, whatsoever things are just, whatsoever things are pure, whatsoever things are lovely (in the Greek the words are 'very lovely'), whatsoever things are of good report; if there be any praise, think on these things."* (Phil. 4:8)

NOTE

1. See *Titles of the Triune God*, H.F. Steveson (Revel).

CHAPTER

7

Weaknesses endured and overcome in Suffering

T hat strength of God comes to us at our lowest to present us at our loveliest. All the promises of God are at work to cause the flame of devotion in your heart to ascend again, and for a sacrifice to be on that flame.

Suffering can reduce the flame, lower the oil content, and place us in a position of absolute helplessness, where even help seems beyond our reach. God is always looking forward, and He reaches towards us, and if grace is not enough, if that ability of God seems to fall short, then God has extra resources to do abundantly above all we can ask or think. Even your meditations can miss the mark in this.

God's love, working hand in hand with his ability, always restores hope, and keeps it alive. Into the dark shadows, a light begins to burn. Sickness can result in death, but even that death, as guided by God can become a gentle breeze, which doesn't blow us out, but produces a fuller and better life in the realms beyond this life, which has been as a smoking flax. God never blows the candle out, but in reality, he grants it such a light as shall never go dim or go out.

✤   ✤   ✤

There is no more apt description of human suffering and burden bearing than the wick which is ready to be extinguished, in Matthew 12:20. Give it all up and leave it all alone. There are desperate moments when the darkness is so deep that the very light which should be ours holds no door ajar for us to enter into the sunlight. Life can diminish your flame. Your desire can be choked to death, even as the seed in the Parable of the Sower. The very happenings of life can take all your reserves until you are as a wick without depth of oil. You were created to give light and to glow, but now your desperate need is for light.

The smouldering wick will only produce that which the old candles used to produce as they burned very low and were about to be extinguished for ever — a dim light leading to a nasty smell. There are so many happenings in life, some so very difficult to handle, and they leave you like a naked flame with a full force seven wind blowing against you. That gusting wind which was meant to be harnessed into a flame has worked in the opposite way and you are left with a smoking flax. God meant it for good, but it has been taken for evil. The ministry is only missed when it burns not. When we begin to stumble we know there is a need for more light which will remove all the questions and doubts. Light was created to transform the darkness, to be a beacon of warmth and radiance, a wick bearing a crown of flame.

Your weakness doesn't destroy the will of God

What can re-spark that smouldering collapsing wick which has known life in its fulness and now is diminished as if an unseen hand has turned it down to a place wherein it is about to be buried? There had once been evidence of a brightly burning fire, its ministry complete. Men and animals had blessed it for showing the way in the dark. Now its unity has been dissolved. Once the wick, the oil, the lamp and the flame worked together and all was well, but the moment we lose our depth of desire then individuality comes to the fore. The smoke and the wick becomes like a Church in schism, just a little bit of wick with a lost ministry and a lost hope. It has come to its hour of darkness. How shall it pray? Father, deliver me from this hour? No, let me drink the cup and let God take the situation and blow the smoking expression into something new, a new flame. The Master alone can replace the wick, pouring in the oil, cleansing what is already there and leaving it shining in its small corner. A flaming wick is a lamp of testimony of triumph. The flame is the evidence of the coronation of the oil and the wick, ignited and aflame. Paul reminds Timothy to "stir" up the gift of God, to fan it into a flame, return to the hand which is able to brighten your past with a brilliant future (2 Timothy 1:6). The Presence of Jesus moving around in the life as He moves around in the midst of the seven Golden Candlesticks in the Book of Revelation can breathe again on that which is ready to die (Revelations 1:13). God blows upon the embers and the delight is that of seeing a roaring fire where once there was ashes and dust and the twigs of yesterday's dreams all burned up and destroyed. Flames, on some altars, can turn cold stones into heat, can lead to sacrifice. Israel could only perform their duties before God when the fire was lit and the candlesticks gave out light, illuminating the fellowship. A new fire! A new flame! There are possibilities here! Something lost can be found, that which is asleep can be disturbed, that which is dim can be brightened and what has not yet been accomplished can be. Everything can be seen by the light of a new fire, kindled by the kindly Christ.

The two on the road to Emmaus came into this revitalisation, *"Did not our hearts burn within us while He talked with us by the way?"* (Luke 24:32). They had experienced a sadness, a slowness of heart, and now through Christ's Presence they became the Knights of the Burning Heart. When Jesus spoke of His Second Coming He drew a picture of a waiting servant with loins girded about and with a lamp which was burning.

The only sure thing in weakness is the whole armour of God

There are periods when we all pass through greater and lesser light, sometimes moments of absolute fulness of light, but also occasions of dimness of sight, when we cannot tell whether it be Esau or Jacob (Genesis 27:22). Hours when we are blinded and have to be led by the hand to the street called Straight. There is a pure devotion which burns, just as first love for Christ does. The command is that the fire on the altar shall never go out. We commence the Christian journey with a flaming torch, but as the years go by it seems to get a little dim. There is hope for all who come within the scope of the fire gone out and the cold altar, for did not Jesus meet the disciples in John 21:9 with a rekindled fire? Even after Peter had been found warming himself near the fire, Jesus steps in to rekindle that desire. When we have toiled all night and have taken nothing, when we feel that

God's plans for our lives lie smashed at our feet with pieces too many to count, our reserves all used up, it is then that we need Jesus to start a fire. Paul, in Acts 28:3, on the Island of Mileta, made a diminished fire burn brightly. After shipwreck and storm the broken bits were placed on the fire and it burned brightly. Because of this a revival came to the island. God, with us, can use part of the wreckage of life to commence a new fire. The tumbles of life certainly take the spark from us. God does not leave us, He seeks us among the ashes of our own abandonment. Benson Idahosa[1] in his book *Fire in his Bones* writes that, as a child, he was abandoned and was found on a rubbish heap... *"the bundle on the rubbish heap began to wriggle"*. The first chapter is called *"A Son Salvaged"*. When we come to the dunghill, thrown out like ashes, when life has so treated us that we have been turned into a cinder of what we once were, then the story will take a strange turn and the power of God and His Gospel which transforms us into something quite beautiful will appear. What a name to have! *"Cinders."* That sums up what can happen in life, how we can become charred and shrivelled, in body and spirit. Once you realise that you were made for the fire you cannot live in the smoke! Being a smouldering wick is being less than you were created to be. There is a certain hypocrisy about smoke, for it is not the real thing it was intended to be! We can be robbed of the flame, the keen edge of the Spirit, that spiritual glow, that bright light in the shining eye, that which depicts zeal, is a burning flame.

In Matthew 12:20 the restoring ministry of Jesus Christ is described. He it is who pours in the oil and the wine. It is the work of Jesus as an Advocate, a Friend working as a Priest, whose ministry included the lighting of the lamps, the cleansing of the wicks, with the replenishment of the oil. That soothing, reaching, teaching, healing, helping, restoring ministry, that which freshens us into another dimension. God can dip us as someone dried out, a smoking flax, into another measure of joyful oil.

Being certain of God's light

When the Lamp of the Lord went out in Israel they knew things were pretty bad. 1 Samuel 3:3... " *'Ere the lamp of the Lord went out"*. Suffering, exhausted by the burdens and heat of the day, the frustrations of the hour, burden upon burden until the donkey cannot be seen for the burdens it carries. All can result in the smouldering wick and the diminished flame. I begin to turn inward. I become inward looking. My usefulness is limited. The halo of light which should have been becomes a garment of darkness. Light will go where it is directed, but smoke will not, it will drift the way of any old wind, and into anyone's eyes making them weep, irritating nostrils and bronchial tubes. So many things in life will turn the lamp down, yet so few that will cause it to burn brightly. The wick needs its radiance restoring. It needs a flame like a laughing face placing on it. Internal combustion needs to become external, transforming it into living fire.

As children we told ghost stories, turning the lights down or out altogether to make the stories more authentic. The shadows became longer, the eyes dimmer until we could actually see the things we were inventing! Familiar objects became objects of terror and of fear. The flower of the day became the lion of the night! An empty bag moving along in the dim light took on different shapes — a lamb, a wolf, a tiger, a snake — creating terror. Life is like that. The unreal can become so real, whilst the real becomes unreal.

The light of love restores us

In Holman Hunt's painting of Jesus Christ which is based on Revelation 3:20, Jesus appears outside the door knocking gently on it. There is growth around the door as if no-one has been in or out for a long time. No light shines in the window. The door is solid and it is shut. It has no small glass window. Wait — there is a lantern in the Hand of Jesus Christ. He knocks with one hand, and in the other He holds the light He intends to bring in with Him when the door is opened. The admission of Christ means the admission of the light. Those flames which surrounded the Law and crowned Sinai until it appeared as a furnace, through grace can be condensed into a lamp. Having a light burning as a flame makes you part of greatness, part of the burning bush ministry. The sun is in the head of the match.

The first thing we do when we arrive home at night is to switch on the light. That is the first thing Jesus Christ does for us, and He floods the whole of the house, the far corners, with the living light of His Presence. The darkness, the despondency only serves to heighten the light as it shines so gloriously once again. The Philippian jailer who was won to Christ through an earthquake, called for lights (Acts 16:29). Then they preached Christ and all His healing qualities into him! He took Paul and his companions and bathed their wounds, but Paul had caused a light to be lit which would never go out. God's answer to a world which is cold and dark, without form and void, is light. Light which the darkness comprehends not.

The trials of life never defeat the triumphs of God

There is a possibility of life losing its moorings and drifting. There are happenings in life that blind the eye and stop the ear. The smouldering wick is represented in all these, but wait a while and Jesus will come again with restored radiance, bringing light again in the upper window, Acts 20:8.

When Abraham was about to make the most noble sacrifice of his life in the slaying of his son, the fire was required. That life of light, love, faith and joy was about to be placed fairly and squarely on the altar and the sacrifice could only be made with fire, as well as with the knife. Genesis 22:6 states, "He took the fire in his hand." Without the blowing on the smouldering wick there is no real sacrifice. We are left with an open vessel which needs refilling. Fire needs to rise from the heart as an act of worship unto Almighty God.

The smoking flax which will not be snuffed out presents us with a figure of that which has been neglected, left alone, maybe to come to where it is in order that God might reveal exactly what He is so that all His capabilities might flow into that wick, reviving it so that it might blaze again with the glory of God. The flame takes the shape of the hand which lit it again. The oil shows the reflection of the face of him who poured it into the vessel. The witness of the man, the spark of life, may have lost its glow, that spiritual glow that Romans 12:11 speaks of — *"Fervent is the spirit"*, — *King James version.* Moffat — *"Maintaining the spiritual glow."* When we are let down, disappointed, downcast, there seems more earth and ash than deep burning conviction.

We can begin again as weakness is perfected by His Presence

We used to gather with Grandad around the fire and from the fire great stories emerged. We sailed on ships of old; we conquered our Mount Everest, and by that same fire we discovered King Solomon's Mines all by ourselves! Dickens had nothing on Grandad when it came to creating characters or presenting caricatures of all he had seen, known or unknown! It was the fire which brought it all tumbling before our eyes like little children in pyjamas tumbling in and out of bed. There, by the light of that fire, the Cavalry rode again, and goodness only records the number of Indians and Indian Chiefs who bit the dust in the shadows of that fire! It was the fire which brought these testimonies to the fore, the flame was something of a general leading into battle, sounding the Charge of the Light Brigade! We saw it all happen before our very eyes, created by the fire!

The older generation of course had their own interpretations of what the fire meant. They could tell the weather, they suggested certain things happening within the fire meant that a stranger was coming to the house. If the ashes fell suddenly, there was going to be a disaster! They even had their own interpretation of what was meant if the flames went to the right or the left of the grate!

God has placed the sun, which is full of light and burning gasses in the sky and in that same sky we have stars which seem like little holes in a cloth letting the light through, and that same God is able to stop the smouldering flax from smelling as it does. The same God can turn it into something bolder by allowing the fires of compassion and understanding to burn brightly again. Jesus will not tread on that which has been trodden on. He will not push down that which is already down. God steals no flowers from coffins! He has no glory in that which dies at His feet. There must be a ministry of healing, flowing from the breath of God which can lift us up again as a flame emerging from a dead fire.

The true marks of gentleness in any greatness

A smoking flax He will not douse. Notice the gentleness of His approach, the stimulation, the Christ with eyes of fire peering into that smoky hold and causing the wick to burn again. Pouring in the precious substance it needs to keep it going as a flaming torch, a testimony to light and life. He does not polish the lamp, the wick is not cut or the vessel turned upside down. There is no walking around it, no charging the lamp with folly. He does not say, this is just what you deserve. No. There is such understanding, such love, such compassion that the lamp feels surrounded by that which it needs. The Creator of fire is here. The Gardener of the Burning Bush stands nearby. The One Who made Sinai catch light is about to step in. He is the God of Fire, the One Who made it all possible. He is the Charioteer of the chariot of fire which caught Elijah away to Heaven, and He answers by fire (2 Kings 2:11; 1 Kings 18:38). The fire is an expression of His Person. The lamp realises this and flames again in an act of worship to the God of the fire. It wants to illuminate the Personage Who has come back into its presence. This little sick bed, the lamp with the smelly wick, is turned into a place of light, a palace of purity, the dawn of a new day. It becomes the talent of the Lady with the Lamp, Florence Nightingale. Your life has been as this lamp, and your life shall be as this lamp now is! The Master has come and He calls for you! The fire which was nearly out, was useless, forgotten, suddenly rises again. Things are as they were and suddenly it is in the light of His Presence. He becomes lamp to lamp, wick to wick, oil to oil. He is made all things to all men. The light that knew only dimness and darkness now wants to see the face of the Visitor, to have a deeper, fuller, wider gaze so it flames up as it should be. The soldier asleep on guard, with the penalty of death hanging over him, is suddenly roused to duty. Battle orders are presented to him. There is a holy glow restored by the One Who came to help, to bring it in, to caress and to care, until like those Paul knew *"Your care for me has flourished again"* (Philippians 4:10), and like a fresh breath of air it is fed by the oxygen of love, taking the form and the shape that God has designed for it.

God begins with us again as if it was the first time

He chooses many ways to arouse the fire again. He can blow on it; the ashes can be removed; He can start all over again, but He will commence that course of action, no matter how little is left. He takes a flax and from that He brings the smouldering and then the flame. He takes that which was dying and unable to give and causes it to flame again.

As the Missionary was attempting to escape from the natives who were throwing spears at him, someone asked which promise went through his mind at that crisis hour. "None," was his reply. *"I didn't need a promise, the Lord was with me!"*

Mourning can be turned into morning, and beauty for ashes. The oil of rejoicing for the oil of mourning. Suffering and pain can draw the curtains not just across the windows but across our hearts and the blackness is very deep, but when the curtains are opened then everything is revealed in its true light. That which is ailing colours so many things. We are drawn inward like a snail going into its shell and we feel that life is, after all, just a shell. Yet there is so much more radiance for us. The wick which has smoked can still become what it was always designed to be — that with a crown of flame on it, giving light to all. What is a little wick but a piece of cloth which is laughing after being immersed in oil!

God's faithfulness is a source of hope

It is an object of pity this fire which is just smoking, a picture of absolute weakness before men and God, suggesting that what has been is now finished. Jesus refuses to give up. In Revelation 3:20 the Greek tense is *He keeps on knocking*. The same applies to Matthew 7:7. *"Keep on knocking, keep on asking."* He keeps on working, standing, pleading, seeking, until the door is opened to Him, until the hurt is shared with Him. He persists in sharing what we have, even if it is but a few loaves and fishes. He can cause it to be so blessed that it blesses many. The bread can feed and the fish can swim where they would never have gone but for the touch of Jesus Christ.

"I sink in life's alarms, when by myself I stand,
Imprison me within Thine Arms and I shall conqueror be."[2]

For the smoking flax to be revived it does not even need another
light, it is an old light an old flame which is restored. Every light is a
ray borrowed from the sun. Our life is borrowed from Him. If we
concentrate the sun through a piece of broken glass it can cause a
fire. That cutting, hurtful piece of glass can be the means of restoring that flame of the heart. When we are ill, it can be so. As the
smouldering wick discovers a new flame, so we can discover a new
God. The smoke can clear, the breathing becomes easier. As the
wick becomes the throne of the flame, let your life be wick and
Christ your flame. The One Who answers by fire, He is God, the
God of every hurt, of every sickness, of every discouragement. He is
the God of knowledge, of love, of understanding. Crown Him with
many crowns! May that flame be a tongue of fire, rising up to bless
God. Through pain and sickness the fire can rise again and the
phoenix rising from the ashes can be you!

There is an old Yorkshire saying: *"They get on my wick"*. It
means, I am under pressure, they discourage me, they would put my
fire out, they are a burden to me.

The plan and pathway to peace

The same light which we required from men, we require from God,
to reveal to us the nature of the pathway on which we are walking.
We need to know where it is leading, where we are going, whom we
are following and why. A light will make all the difference in the
world. What has been a mountain in the dark may well turn out to
be diamond in the light, the very hand of God which has been
placed there to catch us and keep us all the days of our lives.

While we are as the smoking flax there are so few who will gather
with us. The beetles and the small creatures of earth, the termites
and ants may creep a little closer to share what little warmth is left,
but no-one will come to cook, to receive light, to obtain warmth or
direction from our fire. If they did, then smoke is all they would
receive. There has been an exchange of ministry which needs to be

altered. Things need turning round, more fire, less smoke, more flame and less of that which brings tears to the eyes.

God's gentleness develops God's greatness

There is a third element missing also. There is smoke and flax, but that which would make a trinity is missing, there is no fire. There is a diminishing influence — three have become two and two are likely, at any moment, to become one. Where is the fire? Where is the desire? Has an enemy done this? Has there been such a storm that the fire has been baptised in water? Did someone forget to replenish it in the night? Ah yes, in the dark night when it was needed the most there was no adding to it, only a taking. Did it happen wilfully? Was it by constant neglect? Flax which will not be put out though it is smoking. Flax, much of it from Egypt and from a living tree. Flax, from when we obtain our English word, Linen, formed into a wick and dipped in oil. The oil had not flowed, it had been allowed to face depth with dryness. There had been less coming in than going out. Has life been like that for you? Is discouragement as smoke? There had been no quality and the light began to fail, had it been a leaking vessel, as in Hebrews 2:1, and there had been a leakage which brought it to this place of smoking instead of burning. The oil might have been wasted on other things.

The lamp gives no light, darkness surrounds it, there is a diminishing flame. It is easy to feel this way when we cannot feel the Presence of Christ. Absence makes the fond heart wander! We can be placed in a situation where there is seemingly no Presence of God. The tongues of fire can expire. The roar of the fire which had been able to match the roar of the lion, is no more. It is weak. Like some passing Samson the Philistines are upon it. Its eyes have been put out (Judges 16:21). Lively coals bouncing off the altar are lively no more. The leap and the thrust, the leaping, walking and praising God have diminished into something lukewarm. Jesus does not say it is a failure, therefore reject it. He knows full well that the stone which the builders rejected has become the Head of the corner. He came unto His own and His own knew Him not (John 1:11).

There has to be the gentle breathings, the whisperings of God to revive it again. He blows again and again, not to blow the house down but to build the flame up, to bring about a resurrection, restoring it to its former glory. Jesus Christ is able to do that.

From all that has taken place in your life, God wants to give fire, zeal and devotion a place to fully express itself. May your tongue be as a burning flax, hot for God. Whatever caused the flame to burn out or turned the wick low must be defeated, so that out of weakness strength may appear again. The smoke must be cleared away to enable everything to be clearly seen. The flame must rise up and take its stand in the lamp as a rag of fire. You must go on in the strength of the Lord.

When Elijah asked the Widow of Zarepath for a morsel of bread and a little water she was gathering sticks to bake a cake with oil and then the fire would go out, for they had no more use for it since their provisions had diminished into a mere handful (1 Kings 17:12, 13). It was a dead cause, as if it had never happened. In a miraculous way God arranged it that the fire stayed burning brightly much longer than the widow ever thought it could. God does those things which encourage us to burn as brightly as a shining light. Every miracle of Christ's restores borrowed rays.

The Glory of God is to receive and revive

Is there another thought in the phrase, "The smoking flax He will not snuff out?" Has the shepherd been here? The sheep have spent the night and they have turned into another way, going forward into a new day and a new pasture. That is not the story of the smouldering flax. The sheep are being led by the shepherd. Later, the fire is discovered by someone else, it having lasted throughout the dark night and has now developed a smoking cough. The fire was made from the flax plant. The real majesty of the moment is to bring it back to life. Let there be a resurrection! The shepherd on his knees blowing into the heart of that which is now cold but which once was hot. It is revived! The crown of flame is restored, there is no need of the flint. There is no requirement of extra oil to be poured on to it. The need is for breath from another realm, a softness which will result in new life which is flame shaped and burning, a ministry to others. The shepherd is now warming himself and his sheep where others were once warmed. The old fire has become a new fire, the shadows chased away by the dramatic appearance of the flames. While the flame was low every movement of tree or branch seemed to be a lurking beast ready to spring. Now it is taken by the throat and destroyed in the new found day and life of the smoking flax. The message is an all consuming one. I rule, here! Within its realm all are safe, all is sure, all is revealed. The new flame is the dawning of a new day, and it all happened because another sheep keeper bent his back and came down to the level of the smoking flax, just as Jesus Christ did for us. The Psalmist, in Psalm 119:83 saw himself as a bottle dried up in the smoke, needing to be filled afresh. It is without capacity, this smoking flax. The shepherd repeats the words of Psalm 4:8:

> *"I will both lay me down in peace and sleep, for thou, Lord, only makest me to dwell in safety."*

The fire has been stirred, it has a lot of burning still to do. It will consume the fuel even as the wick drinks the oil. There is so much for us to enter into through God. God hasn't finished with you yet! There can be another roaring flame, more conquering of the darkness, another opportunity to be dipped deep into the oil. The gentle handling and breathings of Christ puts everything back into its proper order. Genesis is beginning all over again. I am returned to where I belong, to do that which I can do best. Here is burning, illuminating, shining, a reaching up into Everlasting Life.

NOTES

1. Benson Idahosa, preacher to many thousands of people and senior minister of Miracle Centre, Benin City, Africa. *Fire in his Bones* (Bridge Publishing and Valley Books, Gwent, UK).

2. "O love that will not let me go," hymn by the blind composer, George Matheson. *Redemption Hymnal*, no. 571 (Assemblies of God, 106/114 Talbot Street, Nottingham NG1 5GH).

CHAPTER

8

The Bruisings and Blessings of Suffering

The metaphor is changed from a smoking wick to a bruised reed. They present to us two different aspects of suffering. One is ready to splutter out, while the other is in a constant state of hurt. One needs something pouring into it, while the other needs a little more shaping.

There are those who only see life in a cloud of smoke. There are others who for ever feel the bruises of a heavy hand, not of grace, but of seeming judgement.

Your life can be that bruised instrument, which love seeks to take again, and cause the music of salvation to sound out as it used to. There is nothing like suffering, bruising and hurt to stop that ministry for the Master. It is good to realise if we have been tripped up, we land in the Everlasting Arms for our everlasting good. The hands that take hold of you contain all the aromatic oils and therapy you require for this bruising.

The bruised reeds of life, of which you may be one, can be a matter, not of just physical pain or hurt, it can be spiritual. There can be bruising within. It can represent silent hurt and suffering. You can seem to lack a place to give expression to your grief. The hand of Jesus, to place yourself there is the best place to give expression to your feelings of remorse and rejection to find a ready remedy in your Redeemer and Friend. To be near Him is to hear His weeping, to feel His caring compassion.

* * *

The smoking flax can send out distress signals through its billowing smoke, calling to someone to revive it with a sweet kiss of life, to revive its resignation. The smoke can do the talking for it. It ascends, and help is despatched to fan the wick until it bursts forth into flame. No such ministry is deposited with the broken reed — Matthew 12:20. It is empty. Out of the hands of the shepherd it is quite useless. It has neither hammer qualities nor rod or staff ministrations. It was deprived of what little it possessed when it fell and was bruised, and it has no means of crying out for help. There can be no shedding of tears. Its emotions are dried up. It is shut off in the darkness like a prisoner condemned, even as Jesus Himself was, without a trial. Dropped from a dizzy height it has no wings with which to fly. Its power to attract has been rudely taken and it can utter no cry for help.

When bruising is so deep we cannot speak

If the bruised reed could shout for help, that shout would be drowned in the depths of the bleating of the sheep. It can only lie motionless, hoping that the sun does not shrivel it up. It is noiseless and harmless, the voice it possessed through its music has been torn from it and it is an empty reed waiting to be crushed into the dust by the many feet which will be planted onto it as if they were working a treadmill. It was as if no man cared for its soul. The reed is as that which is thirsty and cannot be watered, hungry and cannot be fed. There is no tune to fill the hollow parts that others cannot reach. The hollowness and emptiness can only be filled by the breathings of its maker and player.

The bruised reed and the smoking flax are beautiful emblems of God's gracious, gentle and patient spirit with which He deals with us. It is not the spirit of the Law, belching fire with trumpet blasting at Sinai, where man is burned to a cinder or thrust through with a dart if he touches the mount, it is the spirit of the Cross, of Calvary. It is the gentleness of Jesus which makes great. We see here the power of God at work helping that which cannot help itself. Its very weakness is the means of bringing glory. It has no power but His power, no ability but His ability, no music but that which the Master gives. Its happy days, its play days, its days of rejoicing, skipping and dancing are its music days, its Red Letter days. The Festive Season, the Last Day at the Proms. Life is music, life is a lilt, it is a golden melody to the reed. It lives, moves and has its being immersed in music. It was created for the score.

Help required can seem far removed

When a person passes through certain illnesses and burdens become the order of the day, the dark clouds gather and the sun that shines above the clouds is forgotten, but the sun remains as it always was, in spite of the clouds or the rolling thunder threatening a storm. There are some sicknesses which seem to cut you off from God and from man. Your emotions become as unstable as water. The tide flowing in and out describes that which is happening in your life, and it is no holiday. Where and when you once felt God and knew the light of His Presence, now you feel only the darkness of His absence, your constant cloud. Like a musical instrument with a bent tube or broken string you have been placed on one side, nothing rings true. There are discordant notes which have been placed within.

A nervous disorder, a mental illness, even an operation can leave you in a state of weakness, as a straw blowing in a fierce wind ready to bend even further, so low that breaking point appears to be very near. Those things which were once a delight to your heart, those thrills of the consciousness of God have shrivelled up and are but cinders of a former fire. You are as one left bleeding and dying on the Jericho Road, out of tune, and the Hand which stretches out has not reached you to save you from falling (Luke 10:30, 34). We are so bruised, so empty, so forlorn that it hardly seems worth taking another step. Each obstacle is a mountain. The mist and the cloud become permanent rock, and we strike against it. In losing sight of what I am following, I lose my footing. The sure places and things of life become uncertain. When all these clouds gather, God provides a silver lining. All the colours of the rainbow are heightened more than ever with the word from the lips of a loving Lord, a Lord Who not only knows the situation, but Who has been bruised just as you have been. He has known all the colours of the bruising. Whatever the length or the load of the Cross, Jesus Christ Himself and not another has been stretched upon it. His body has covered it. He has entered into the darkness. Through His Resurrection and the rolling of the stone away, Jesus has put a light where once darkness and ignorance had their strongholds. They have bowed to Him. He wears their crown among the many crowns upon His head (Revelations 19:12).

Pain can be heard and interpreted

What is bent, He will not bend further. The only time God bends us is to shape us into a situation which will cause us to be fully used by Him. There has to be a rounding to the bend and a squaring to the corner. That which is down He will not throw down. God does not drop the weight of hell upon you whilst you are down like some wrestler falling upon his opponent, or the hammer-head going into the brag nail. He does not bruise further or deeper. God will never hurt the hurt or sting the stung. There is a whole area of encouragement if we are seeking the pathway back to health. He will travel with us and show us the way. The unsure step, the weak faith, the dim light, the broken reed will all be taken care of by the capable Hands of Jesus Christ. All He asks is that we trust Him. As people came to the carpenter's shop with their broken wheels, snapped axles, rotting boards and broken carts and handed them to Joseph and Jesus to mend, so He would ask that we trust Him in these dark situations. That which had fallen apart and was worthless was made into workable worth, that which was useless was restored.

John 3:16..."That they might not enter a place of uselessness." We need to function as a reed sounding out music. I want to be what God has created me to be — a Christian. I would make a very poor atheist! I want to fully find and to be fully formed into what God has designed. I don't want to perish in the using of my life. The Shepherd with the lost sheep looked for it on and behind every hill, and thus God seeks for us. There is something ever-seeking and everlasting about the love of God. You can never fall below it or rise above it. You cannot drift beyond His love and care. Even in a valley you will find a mountain of love. There is that content of the love of God which will be reserved until we are found. Then, and only then, the content will be emptied into our lives, healing the hurt, binding up the broken hearted, bathing the bruise in blessing.

The bruised reed He will not break. There are those things in life which we rub against which bruise us and hurt until we become a whole hub of hurt. Life is a metal object which falls on us and hurts. Like the man in the story of the *Good Samaritan* (Luke 10:30), we fall among thieves. The thief comes to rob, kill and destroy, but Jesus has come that we might have life. The thief will break through and steal, but we need that which the thief cannot steal, the very thing which moth and rust cannot touch, things not related to the body but deeper, more sure, everlasting pearls which are part of our spirit. The only real security for these things is to give them back to God (Matthew 6:19, 20).

There is a certain violence about sickness. There is an horde, an army which rides in and plunders leaving us feeling raped. The things we prized and held dear are taken with such great violence. It is as if a volcano which we have been living close to erupts and all that we have trusted in is shaken and buried in ashes and lava. It is as the midnight hour, the heart is left empty, the children which were ours are not, the preciousness and sanctity of life has been violated. The story of the bruised reed which will not be broken is your story. It is the story of the sickbed. It acts for us like the nearness of the nurse. We become part of every sufferer. You can take heart from the sayings of Jesus and every word can become a balm which melts gently over the sore area until the healing takes place and we are strong and well and whole again. The reed has belonged to the shepherd, but it is now bruised. His greatest joy is to restore it to its former glory.

We all require a helping hand

The reed had grown by the water's edge. It could be found in plant life. Then one day someone came by and, with a knife, simply cut it from the main stalk. The scenes once enjoyed were going to be different. It was going to travel as part of the shepherd's equipment for soothing and rejoicing. It was going to be a comforter for the dark and lonely nights which lay ahead. Dark valleys and weary pastures

would hear its music. That hollow instrument, a reed, not now blowing in the wind but playing in the wind, music from the mouth of the
instrumentalist, a musical instrument in the hands of the shepherd.
It was more than a plant for decoration, or a plaything of Mother
Nature. That lathe-like knife would do its hurting, shaping, sharing
work, creating the instrument. The cutter became the designer. He
wanted to make an instrument out of the reed. That simple hollow
tube was changed by the shepherd working on it and shaping it. The
breath of that same shepherd could take it on into a new ministry. It
had been taken from a stable stagnant life and a new ministry was
to become its end.

The guide knew the correct size and shape. The sharpened knife
peeled away any spare form until it was the right length and shape,
until it fitted both hands and lips perfectly. It was his musical box,
the equivalent of our modern radio.

God creates His own music within us

The reed was unlike the rod or the staff. It was not an instrument of
war other than in the sense that the bandsman is part of the war
effort. This small reed would not aspire to great heights. It knew its
place. It needn't strive to become something else, it had to be just
what the master had made. It would never sound the charge, as the
bugle did. It couldn't soothe, as the harp or the violin. That did not
matter, there was a purpose for its existence. The shaping was the
work of the shepherd. On the lonely and dark nights, nights so quiet
and still, nights where the blackness could be felt, out there in the
black jungle of night the reed and the shepherd would join together
in harmony — his breath, lips and hands, the reed's hollow tube,
working together in unity to bring about music which could destroy
melancholy and depression; music which would open doors in brick
walls and send mountains rolling like rubber balls, the shepherd
blowing on the tube until music sounded out from valley and hill.

David had his harp, but most shepherds had this much cheaper
instrument which was easy to carry, to play, to listen to, but also
easy to lose in the rush and bustle of life. The sheep were mesmer-
ized by the playing of music from the reed. It was a lovely change

from the monotonous sounds of the night, and from their bleatings. The bleating of sheep was all on one note, the music from the pipe was different. It had a scale, a range all of its own. What was naked, lonely and sometimes eerie was filled with a soul soothing song from the reed, created and creative in its music. There were now songs along the dusty pathways they travelled, and musical notes were there to cheer. March tunes helped them to move along. It meant that no two nights would be the same. Every day a new melody came from the heart of the reed. It added colour to that colourless drab contour. There wasn't a sweeter or more reassuring sound than the songs of the pastoral pipe. Through its melodies scenes opened up like the pages of a story book. Old lovers and happenings were all brought to life as if from a magician's hat. Scenes of childhood and of boyhood, emotions came into the dark valley filling it with light, hope and cheer. When the way was weary, dark and dreary the music lifted the foot higher and caused it to walk over any obstacle. Spirits were lifted by an unseen hand into a higher realm. When the hands hung down and the feeble knees were ready to droop it was the music of the rush which turned them back into the way. It was the voice and the heart of the shepherd who went in and out among the sheep with these beautiful sounds. Many a shepherd was known by the tunes he played on his rustic pipe.

Let go and let God act on your behalf

Like the notes of a piano emerging from the hands of the musician, its ministry ceased. The darkness enveloped it. It was in a large place and was so small a thing, so insignificant, who would miss it? Who or what would care for it? There were so many other reeds, stalks to be trimmed and pared by the knife, taken up.

The reed would be carried in the girdle of the shepherd. It could not walk or beg. It was carried where it could hear the beat of the shepherd's heart, in fact the music which came from it was a translation of the heart beats, the moods and the emotions of the shepherd. The pipe was the voice of the shepherd in music form. It was kept near the shepherd's bag containing his food. Music was next to food. As the man did his work, as he moved to feed and to attend to the lambing, the reed was wrenched free from its hold. It may have happened as he was lifting a lamb, but there was that final jolt, causing it to leave the side of the shepherd. It fell to the floor with a light fall as it was worked loose in the activity. Little by little it was brought to the edge of the precipice, one moment safely tucked into the girdle, the next slipping until it floated to the ground.

We are bruised by many a fall and slip

It fell into a bed of sickness. The fact of the fall had jolted all the music from it. Insult was added to injury as it lay there in the mud without the breath and the lips and lacking the hands of manipulation. The animals with their many hooves trod on it, bruising it even more.

Who would want a bespattered instrument such as this, clothed in mud and fixed fast to the face of the earth, bruised and, in its own way, bleeding? Whoever would want such a trophy as this? The very need for its existence ceased to be. Its sun set whilst it was still day. In the light of the day, midnight came. All its usefulness had gone. Feelings were buried, crushed under temptation, lost in the wild wilderness, not thrown down or out deliberately, but just let slip. What happened was not a cunningly devised plan, it was no fable. No foot flattened it. No flood overwhelmed it. It was among the flock, being trodden on, bruised, flattened. Perhaps the next thing to stand on it would break it forever. The loneliness, the heartache, the separation from the sheep and the shepherd, the songs replaced by sighs and dejection. The thought of utter rejection was there. As Paul said, "Lest I myself become a castaway" — a rejected vessel (1 Corinthians 9:27). The usefulness would be diminished beyond recovery. You cannot mix mud with music! There are no scales in sludge and slime. In the bruise there is no harmonious band playing.

Happiness and helpfulness seem to disappear

All the reed can think about is its bruises. It can remember the happy music, the delightful melodies, yet they are but a muddy memory now. The music is lost in the fall of the pipe, it is buried with it. It is but a shallow grave hidden in the grasses. The shepherd's symphony will remain unfinished forever! That which was pieced together, note by note, both sheep and shepherd, is no more. There had been that in it which could outsing the birds. It had trilled its music into tree and flower. Who will pity the abject article now? If it had been a gun or a knife, some cannon or missile of war, even if it had been but an axe head, they might have asked "Where fell it?", searching for it, but nobody would enquire about a reed which was bruised. Other holes had now been opened up in its side, alongside those made by the designer — sores which had been gathered by the fall to the earth. It was more like a pin cushion than a music pipe. It lies there in its forlorn blackness. It can never hope to grow again, its roots were severed when the instrument maker took it and fashioned it. The only stroke, the only touch it will know now is the howling wind, the kiss of the sunbeam or the sniff of a marauding animal who will sense that it has been among the sheep. If only it had a voice to call for help. The only noise that would be created is if the wind were to blow and a moaning sound might then come from it. It would sound ghostly and might frighten rather than be a friendly sound. It lies as a coffin now, rather than as a musical instrument. It left the shepherd's side and in doing so, it died.

The helplessness we all feel

Did it hear the footsteps of the shepherd? No; it was only the howling wind sounding the death dirge over it. If only it had fallen where sunlight could bathe it back to health. Even if it had fallen into the river there was the slight chance that it might be carried downstream and there be seen, lifted out and restored. If it had fallen on the main thoroughfare there could be a possibility that another shepherd would find it. Had it fallen near to a well or some other oasis that would have increased the hope of its being found.

The shepherd wants to play his music. The nights are long, black and lonely. The sheep are resting and the fires have descended into a rich ruby glow. All is still. The wolves may come soon. The lion may spring a surprise. The shepherd must keep awake, the watch must be kept for the safety of the sheep. What shall he do to combat the boredom? He throws pebbles into a pool, he tries practising with his sling ready for an unseen attack, he plucks the leaves from the stem in his hand, he begins to think of his wife and family at home, he remembers Temple Worship — how he wishes that he could be there, singing the lusty glorious songs of Zion! All these things creep over his soul as moonlight creeps over the landscape, bathing it in soft light. In the darkest night at the darkest point he will play a little music that will keep him awake and arouse his soul. He may even pretend he is not a shepherd at all, in the lilt of the music in the moonlight he may even think that he is a priest, a soldier, a ruler, a king. Hadn't King David dreamed like this? He reached for his pipe, that trusty musician by his side, that orchestra in one small instrument. It was not there! Music shrivelled into an empty grasp of air, disappeared into cloth girdle. A robber has been! Someone has stolen my prized possession! Am I dreaming? I must not fall asleep within myself. He felt again, the pipe had gone!

The shepherd begins to search. He has to look even more keenly than when seeking a sheep. Swinging his light this way and that he seeks the pipe. It must be found! He retraces his steps. He has lost a precious jewel yet, if he finds it, it may be so crushed and split that it may never again be fit for use, but he must have his music, it must sound again within his ears! The feelings of his heart must flow again through that hollow tube. When did he last use it? Which pastureland last heard the strains of the song? Did he have it when he climbed that last hill? Was it then that it fell from his side? Such questions can only be answered when he finds the reed.

He spends many hours searching among the sheep. Was it lost among friends and sought for sorrowing, like Jesus Christ? (Luke 2:48). Fancy it falling among the sheep, right where all the activity has been! He finds it where it fell, unmoved, untouched, unplayed, it has remained there cold and silent as death and the grave.

Warm hands are placed around the reed, the strength it needs is placed around it to bring it close to the leader's heart of love. It can be carried along again. It is to be placed at his lips. It will see the smile and know the joyous face again. O, the potential of the shepherd's hands, not just to cut and carve, but to care and to show compassion, to lift and to love, to play again, to give a new song. It is back where it belongs, bloodied but not bowed. Now, after the finding will come the fixing. Whatever happens it knows it will be for the best, administered through the hands of its keeper, finder, player and friend.

There is healing for our bruising

The glory of any shepherd is to find a bruised reed and still to get music from it. Bruised and twisted it is hurt and harmed. It reminds us of the famous Paganini who, whilst playing his violin, felt first one string then another break until he was left with but one, yet he continued playing until the end of the performance. He commented, "Paganini, and one string!"

The shepherd could have taken another piece of reed and created a new pipe, but he loved the feel of it in his hands — this pipe had been his companion, he had many memories enshrined in it. Another reed would be like a stranger, a cold tool, rather than a musical instrument.

It is badly bruised. The natural reaction of many would be to break it in two and throw it away, even further than before, so that it sinks from sight. This is not the mind of the shepherd. It is not his theology at all. The flag is picked up to be waved again in triumph. He cleans it, blows upon it with the same gentle breath as he blew on the smoking flax. The dust and the dirt are removed. Any foreign bodies are conquered with the sweep of his hand. He may even wash it in a stream. He may be so overjoyed at his success that he lets his tears trickle over it, washing it. There is a light in the eyes of the herdsman. Joy has returned and is hoisted as a flag from a castle wall. That which was lost is found! Rejoice with me! The taunt has been to sing or to sound out the songs of Zion whilst laying abandoned on the ground...now that taunt can be answered with a melody. He may have to make new holes in it to sound out the true tune. There must be a new piercing process. He takes it and out of disaster triumph is born, with love. That which is bruised and battered is taken and it is tried again, and once again becomes the organ in the wilderness, the reed of recital.

Bruising has a way of composing its own music

At first the sounds are a little off-key, as if it was created before music was invented! To the passer-by it might sound as if a throat is being slit, as if it is all puff and blow from the keeper of the sheep and no other sound is heard, but by constant application, new holes are made and the songs are restored.

The fall, the frailty, the bruising have done something to the music. Where it was superficial before it is now deep and resonant, there is a new depth. Whilst lying on its back in the mud it has learned the new lesson of the raindrop, cloud and storm, the hard frost, the cold wind and the beating hoof. All these things have been its schoolmasters. It has been hammered and nearly smashed and during that time something has entered into its soul which has mellowed it. Like Joseph in prison they put him in irons (the margin of the *King James Bible* says, "they put iron into his soul" (Psalms 105:18)). The music now has a golden ring about it. It gathered something, even as a diamond does from the dark. There were lessons in the mud which had to be learned, things it would never have been taught among the sheep or by the shepherd's side. There was something in the mud which spoke into it and made it into a more useful instrument. The leader of the sheep now finds that he can play deeper tunes and he can reach higher notes on the reed than ever before. It is as if its range has been stretched and there is a whole new scale and range which has been placed into it that talking, hammering, beating or threatening could never have accomplished. The loss, the fall, the bruising and the blackness, the separation have all done a work of worth and glory. Glory has been added to its dimensions. They have played music into the reed and it now has a new legacy which it can pass on to others. The reed has become the silent listener and learner. The shepherd knows the story fully of the bruised reed which was found, rescued and restored.

Poets[1] have suggested that, when we burn wooden logs, the noises of the juices coming out under the heat are really long ago conversations of lovers, and also noises of birds or the falling of the fruit and berries from the trees. The sound of the stream with its own music, the choir of the Dawn Chorus. The logs, in their green state, caught the sounds, some discordant, others beautiful and well rounded, and they were all trapped and sealed for many years only to be released at a later date, quite changed, into sounds so different. The rustic sound became the resonant sound. The log in the fire became the pulpit of nature.

How much like life all these things are — the bruised reed, the log in the fire releasing its sounds; they are but a parable of life. Your bruising is the bruising of the reed. Your suffering is the log on the fire, releasing in another form everything which ever happened. The shepherd had great joy in finding the reed bruised and in not breaking it but in taking it up again to be used with fresh music. It was not a new reed, not even an old one done up or taken into another shape, it was a bruised reed with a story to tell. These are parables of life and of human suffering, and they are a part of all of us.

NOTE

1. William Wordsworth, Robert Browning and Rudyard Kipling.

The Loneliness of Suffering

W e are all called to bear it alone. Even when the burden has been shared and halved, there is still a portion of it to be born alone. We are shut in with it, but after the smoking flax has found a new flame, and the bruising has been taken and turned into a tune, then we have realised that we are shut in with God. One of the prevalent sicknesses of the modern world is that of loneliness. It might be your particular wart. The feeling of being a church steeple or a desert island does not escape some of us, in fact, at times it is part of all of us. Some hide it better than others. "My God, my God, why have you forsaken me," was uttered by Jesus Christ in desperate loneliness, that he might understand your loneliness. He felt as desolate as sand and that which is termed barren. Pain and sickness, suffering and a sense of loss can open the door to loneliness. Through that same door, if it is opened wide enough, a Friend can come, who has been knocking in gentleness, and wants to deepen your experience and relationship with himself. He is now shouting in the pain and frustration to be let in. It can happen at any moment. This feeling of isolation, but not having a contagious disease can become part of you. You cannot isolate God of grace in suffering. Here is how it happened to me.

❋   ❋   ❋

There was a noise in the distance. It was not a shout or a voice, it was as if someone was speaking whilst having a mouthful of food. It might have even been the shout of one who was muffled or gagged, or the sound of some distant, roaring football crowd when the goal has at last been scored. The voice came nearer, the sounds taking shape. At the same time lights began to shine in my head and then, as if dawn had suddenly dawned through the darkness, I was conscious. I could hear and see. The noises had been those of the hospital ward going about their daily work. I was on the four posts of sickness lying helplessly after a car accident. This wasn't Heaven. It wasn't hell. It wasn't in-between. "Where am I?" A nurse hurried to my side to comfort me and then it all came back, the accident, the impact, the screeching of brakes, the depth of impenetrable blackness as if a light had suddenly been turned out, black curtains drawn across a window. My eyes felt heavy again as if I was drifting, maybe even falling off the edge of the world and into the blackness of loneliness.

As lonely as an island

As I lay in that sleepy hollow of sickness I began to feel very lonely. It was at that moment that I began to realise just how lonely one can be. How far distance is, how individual individualism is. Loneliness can be a fragment of eternity in a moment of time. There was a permanent horizon between myself and my God, a sort of gaping hole which could not be spanned, measured or filled. It was as if the spanner did not fit around the nut that it was designed to fit. Thoughts began to race through my mind, thoughts as many as sparrows in an English Autumn, gathering together for migration. As these torments came and went there was a real sense of God's Presence stealing over my soul as one sees sunlight kiss a tree or a flower. It was so good, so great, so sweet, to realise that I belonged to God and that God belonged to me! So wonderful to realise that God had not used up all His Presence on others, that the ability of God to draw near had not been withdrawn from His nature. Did it mean that I had not used up all my credits? These emotions, feelings, assurances, call them what you will, began to sink into my spirit, not to disappear but to remain for me to go on in them and in the strength of them for many future days. The Presence of God, between the snowy white sheets, tucked in like a shirt into trousers, seemed to catch what had been falling and the broken pieces were brought together again as a video replayed. All the broken bits of my life were whole again.

I could neither read nor pray. I had no appetite for books of knowledge. The Bible seemed a cover without content. Even when I was prayed for, it didn't seem to matter. There were those who came and went, who prayed for me as I drifted in and out of my little holy bed closet, but everything was quite distant, except this *Friend* called *Assurance*, who came to share the bed with me, my ministering angel, my spirit of grace and word of knowledge during my time of sickness. Sometimes we are so lonely because we let the stresses of life build walls instead of bridges, close doors instead of opening them.

Loneliness has a message for the listening ear

If ever salvation meant anything, it meant everything at this moment. All I had read, listened to or been taught now seemed to matter less and less. It was all so irrelevant and almost irreverent in the situation. There were things which in the past God had placed in me and I had become a well which was about to be turned into a reservoir. That placed in me because of my experiences with God was going to be pulled up from below and within, enriching, ennobling my spirit to help me to rest, not *"in God"* but *"on God"*. As I lay in that bed I must rest in Jesus Christ, almost like the tear resting on the bare cheek. There I lay and there I rested, while the meditations of my heart exceeded the words of my mouth, and were acceptable to my God and my Redeemer. The Word of God became my source of strength, as pillars in weakness and as light during dark hours.

Jesus had said, "I will never leave you nor forsake you" (Hebrews 13:5). I was going to prove the truth of this, and the reality of it would rivet itself in me. I would learn that truth now, not by memory or quotation, not by brainwashing session, but by trial and triumph. Were the everlasting Arms underneath? (Deuteronomy 33:27). Did God? Could God? Was God? There was going to be in me a deeper, larger burning fire. The light of the spark or the glow worm is small, but that within me was going to be stirred up into a bright burning, as a great fire of volcanic measure, the discovery of a lifetime! It was the discovery of me, not by another, but by myself!

The words, *"Man, know thyself"*, were abcut to be fulfilled in my life.

The modern rendering of Hebrews 13:5 brought me an updated commentary: *"I will not leave you in the lurch."* When that comes which knocks not only on the door but knocks you from pillar to post then I will not leave you.

Peter had said, "I will never leave you, even if I have to go to prison" (Luke 22:33). Peter failed. He went to prison alright, but it was a prison of his own making. The door and the bars were cast at his own anvil. Jesus was different from Peter. This, I was finding out.

Loneliness helps us to discover faith and friends

Jesus Christ is different. He does not say one thing and then disappear. Was that true? Would it be true for me in my extremity? What He says, stays. What He has said, is sure. The words of Jesus are words of comfort during a time of bereavement and trial. They echo on in the darkness, abounding in promises of new light — tunnel end promises. I was like Paul who had certain friends who were his comforters, in Colossians 4:9, 10 there was Onesimus, Aristarchus, Mark, Justus, all Paul's comforters. They were like a *Get Well Card.* Their ministry describes an oration from a silver tongue, the tongue of an orator, Tertullian. As they spoke it was as if a sermon was being preached to a congregation — a congregation of one — Me! As a comfort they were *paregoric*, the word used for a branch of drugs, the type of drug which eases pain, the tincture of opium which dulls. To know that Christ is with us in any situation is satisfying indeed. It works wonders in the human spirit. It broadens the mind to accept it. It destroys many a thought which would distract or persuade otherwise. The reason Christ is ever with us (Hebrews 13:5) is because verse 8 states *"Jesus Christ, the same yesterday, today, tomorrow"*. You name the day, the date, the time or the hour, and Jesus Christ is ever the same. We alter, we all have our melting seasons, changing reasons, our moments of sincere doubt, but Jesus Christ remains the same, not the sameness of repetition but the sameness of variety. A flower is a flower, yet all are made so differently. No two human beings are exactly the same, for God has made us all different. Yet in that difference there is a sameness. In Jesus Christ He opens His hand and satisfies the desire of every living thing.

He was opening His hand to me. He was revealing so many things, not as He does now at the moment of activity and soul winning, praying, preaching, but in quiet meditation and in that meditation there was a mediation of quietness. His Essence was distilled into my spirit. That victory of Christ was becoming mine. The love of God was being shed abroad in my heart, even as scented petals were scattered in the Grecian arena to dull the scent of death and blood. It was more than mind over matter, it was God's Mind and my matter. This was Spirit over body, the assurances of Christ reigning supreme in every part of me, in every part of my life. All was left in the love of God to shield, to care, to help in recovery. If I lived, I was the Lord's. If I died, I was His, and He is very much alive! I was a winner on every side. I could hear what He said to my spirit when I could detect no other voice. There was that Holy Presence, like a fragrant ointment, perfuming the whole place, put there in the pain as with soft velvet gentle hands of a child, soothing properties released as I was captivated.

Loneliness doesn't mean God has deserted you

God is wanting to give you a new interpretation of himself. Goodspeed, in his translation, puts it succinctly:

> *"I will never let go of you or desert you."* (Hebrews 13:5)

He is not just going to stand by us, He is going to be the controlling factor, the regulator of every regime, the stabiliser in the storm. The Amplified New Testament: *"I will not in any degree leave you helpless nor forsake you nor let you down."* I was proving this to be true. When knocked off my feet I was finding there was a sure foundation. In falling, I was experiencing a catching. There was that in life which would not let me go. You will not and have not left me in the lurch.

There are some riches of grace which we only discover in extremities, in the deep mines of suffering. There, many a sparkling gem of rare quality is found, ideas and ideals we never bother with until we are placed in a corner facing real crises or danger. As there are reserves in the body for fuel, there are also reserves in the spirit which are brought out when we are knocked out. J.B. Philips gives to us some useful and wonderful words when he translates 2 Corinthians 4:9 — *"knocked down but not knocked out"*.

Loneliness can be a lever into love

When we desire God, even when we desire nothing else, the same truth is brought to us. The word used in Hebrews 13:5, never, is the same Greek word which is used in John 6:35, "He that comes to me shall *never hunger"*. The Book of Revelation adds its own words, *"They shall neither hunger nor thirst anymore"* (Revelations 7:16). He satisfies the soul. He satisfies every part of us. He is able to fill us in every area. Columbus when he travelled the world making new discoveries in the name of Spain, found there were oceans, planets and islands within himself which needed discovering and developing. There are parts of us all which are remote and hidden, where no flag has been erected, where no ownership has been established, an area which has never heard the words *"The Master has come and He calls for you"* (John 11:28). There are parts and paths within our hearts, lonely islands and quays. Be it with the weak hand of sickness, I am led into them, and if it has to be under some burden that I am called to climb higher and go deeper until I discover all the possibilities and reserves which are in myself, then so be it. Let God be God. The deepest need of all of us is to leave our prison of loneliness, to be set free into what is the all of our existence in God. What I am being changed into is the likeness of the I AM. There are many keys which God uses to set us free. That depth, height, length and breadth of the love of God is brought to me and I am brought to it through many avenues, not all of them kissed with brilliant sunshine.

As natural food will fill a desire, so the Presence of Christ will bring us through, satiated and satisfied. Sometimes it is only after an event that we realise He didn't just pull us through or take us through, He walked through with us, until those who had looked on the flames which surrounded us in our trial saw another form likened unto the Son of God (Daniel 3:25).

Loneliness is not good for us

"They all forsook Him and fled. He came unto His own and His own received Him not" (Mark 14:50; John 1:11). They would not share His fellowship, but wanted to retain their aloofness, their loneliness. Loneliness was the first thing which God saw in Creation that was not good — thus Eve was created, to break the monotony and loneliness of Adam. We have to be brought to utter those golden words, "I belong". It is a strange process which, sometimes, makes us thoroughly part of the Divine nature. It is this remarkable released ability of the Suffering Messiah to take care of us on the mountain top, through the valley and over the little hills of life which blends Him with our spirits and makes Him so very precious to each one of us. The gold of Ophir is but rust when compared with His loveliness and beauty. It is revealed many times among the ashes of life — from the ashes the phoenix arises — a whole new person. The one who was so gently placed into the sick bed, it is from the shadows of that one that another steps forward with a shield of gold in His spirit to go forward to conquer. A Eunice (2 Timothy 1:5) — "happy in victory."

When we are physically ill, the pressures become too great for us to bear and we crumble as a biscuit between the fingers, but there is a healing balm which is of greater nobleness than that of Mount Gilead (Jeremiah 8:22), it is the healing which takes place in our spirits. We can be well, physically as sound as a drum, yet beaten very often. There is another side to the coin, there is an inner self which needs the healing that the companionship of Christ brings.

In the English language a companion is, literally, "one who shares your bread". Jesus shared our bread in pain, in suffering, in torment and in torture. He sat under the crown of thorns. That person, that companion, sits where you are sitting, stays where you are staying, rises, eats, sleeps, comes and goes, with you. They are what you are, they become your twin. Jesus Christ is our champion Companion. He comes with bread during a time of hunger. He shares with you what He has and what He is. He is the Bread of Life. There is an old tradition that when the Children of Israel ate manna in the Wilderness, that manna tasted as they wanted it to. Your bread may be stale, dry or hard, a little like the bread of the *Gibeonites* (Joshua 9:5), which was mouldy. His Bread is Heaven fresh! The New Testament word for Companion is "away from one's own people". As in your seclusion you feel away from all your friends, so did Jesus Christ when He came to this earth. He was a stranger, but you took him in. If anyone was away from His own people, it was Jesus, having left Heaven's heights for earth's depths. We have to take a journey of discovery, just as important as Columbus or Marco Polo — it is to discover Christ in all His fulness, so that your forlornness is lost in His fulness. It is the discovery of the ages, an ageless discovery.

You can be so lonely in a crowd

You can be lonely even in the midst of a crowd. You can be in a funeral procession whilst attending a wedding! Life, which was meant to be so large can be so little. It can squeeze you out of your very reason for existing. Wine so easily becomes vinegar. I am always heartened by the words "Jesus Himself drew near" (Luke 24:15). Not as an observer or spectator, a watcher of a game, but it says He went with them. Wherever they were going, He also was going.

> *"What manner of communications are these that you have one with another?"* (Luke 24:17)

The words, one with another, are *"tossing the ball"*. Life was still a ball game. It was dull just throwing the ball to one another. You see, friend, the Batsman called Jesus was out. There was no third party to maintain the conversation, to suggest new ideas or new approaches. There was, when Jesus stepped in and asked about their *communications with one another*. It can be between two but not include Jesus Christ. Friendships can exclude Him. We need someone to pick up that ball, particularly if it was a heavy stone which we are not able to roll away. A one man, one person ball game is not much fun. Being sequestered is like that. Life has to be made up of more than *"Me and my shadow"*. There has to be the enlarging of the inner self to embrace Jesus Christ and all that He is and has.

When the eyes of our spirits are opened to see no man save Jesus only, then true fellowship with Christ is established. Paul, during a crisis when he felt all had forsaken him, said, *"The Lord stood by me"* (2 Timothy 4:17). Stood by me as a man with a light, as John Baptist saw himself standing by Jesus Christ, ready to unloosen the sandals from His feet. Stood by me as a soldier on guard, shoulder to shoulder, making us an invincible force for good and right. Stood by me as a faithful servant, listening and waiting for my faintest whisper. I can be as lonely as the widow's mite, but Jesus added to it with His words of commendation.

Aeroplanes and birds may fly. There are ships which sail. There are things which leave us everyday, but when every one of them has gone and each has put its light out, there is One Who can step into that loneliness and break it forever, lighting such a light that it blazes in the soul and illuminates all the caverns of darkness with His friendship. A friend has been described as "one who steps in when the world steps out".

Loneliness is dispersed by recognised friends

The true ornaments of a house are the friends who visit. The same applies to hospitalisation...the best gift anyone brings to a hospital bed is the gift of friendship and what they leave behind in laughter, joy, sparkle, humour, cheer, kindness and kisses. When leaves are in bud and develop into their fulness outside of the branch they do not forsake the branch, they simply beautify it by stepping alongside. When we feel that God is on one side and we are on the other, it is only that God might do something new for us from a totally different angle. Another aspect, another colour of His love is what God is seeing and working on. There are things which need rounding, things which need squaring, dimensions needing to be elongated, and Christ alongside us is doing just that. There is that beautiful verse in Zephaniah 3:17, *"He will rest in His love"*. There is another rendering, *"He will plan silently for you in love"*. The God

Who appears to be inactive in my loneliness is full of activity, activities which will result in my assurance of His Presence. The best present God can bring to any bed of sickness is the present of His Presence.

It is isolation, leaving us with everything displaced, left all alone. Demas may forsake us. Mark may go to another place, but God will remain where He has been invited. When we have invited Him to be with us, then He will be with us, but not always in brilliant sunshine. Not always there in the cheer, the pat on the back or the smile. The final words of Jesus in Matthew *"Lo, I am with you always"* (Matthew 28:20), means every season, every type of weather. God comes from every thorn and proves He is a rose indeed in our times of need. He is always at work. He travels along our way, but that way includes all His ways, peaceful, easy and pleasant. When Jesus said, *"Take My yoke upon you"* (Matthew 11:29), He meant the words *"My yoke is easy,"* it is well fitting, it will not chafe, it is meant to harness you more closely to Me. God is there with us. If one falls, He holds up. He makes both ends meet in Himself. There has to be such oneness that there is no gap, not even for light or air. We have to become as one nature. There has to be a lining up until you cannot tell where one commences and the other concludes.

Loneliness can be your introduction to love

Our laying on one side is to discover that we have another side, a spiritual side. We are not only flesh and blood. If that were the case then all our injuries would be in the flesh and we know that they are not. There are pangs and pains of the spirit also. It is that we might discover Who it is that really matters, Who we really care about. *"Cast all your care on Him, for it matters to Him about you"* (1 Peter 5:7). God has respect for our human solitariness, that is why Eve was created for Adam. It was not good for man to be alone. God has respect for our spiritual needs and He is fully cognizant with the facts of faith. That is why He sent Jesus to help us. He became a man, flesh and blood and bone, like we are, so that He might be a part of man forever. O to have eyes to see and ears to hear what God is saying to my spirit! What God is placing in my inner self until I

become more strong spiritually than I am physically. Little Paul —
yet how strong he was! Strengthened by might in the inner man.
Romans 16:23, "Quartus, a brother." A small man, meaning a quar-
ter — a small portion, — yet he counted and was mentioned by
Paul.

"I will never forsake you" (Hebrews 13:5) ...the rope to the boat.
"I will never let any slack come between you and Me. There will be
no drifting, no drowning, no sinking, for I will be with you." There
is the idea of never relaxing on your behalf, never giving up on you.
Like some explorer, never saying that there is no more to be discovered or uncovered. Whatever picture feelings paint, somewhere in
that painting you will find My signature. Alfred Hitchcock, the film
producer, always had a part in his own films, disguised as one man,
then another, a paper vendor, a shoe shiner, a barrow boy or even a
passer by. When the disciples were in the boat and it was filling up
with water, they discovered a Jesus in a rocking, sinking boat.
"Peace, be still" (Mark 4:39). His words of assurance — wonder
working words which marshalled the winds and waves as an army
under His command. *Jehovah Shama* — The Lord is there.

This same thought of never leaving or forsaking us, is shown in
Acts 16:26 — *"loosing"* the prisoners chains. Then again in Acts
27:40, used of *"loosing"* rubber bands. God will never get free from
us like that. God never takes you on and then puts you off. You will
never be the old shoe or the old hat. He doesn't take us for a ride
and then, when the hills become steep, says, Sorry, I cannot bear two
of us. I haven't the power to care enough for two. He counts your
uprisings and your downsittings. He counts the stars and names
them. He knows when there is one sparrow less. He counts the hairs
of your head, because you count in every fine detail. You matter to
Him. You are His favourite flavour, his favourite topic, for in His
image and His likeness you were created.

Loneliness can be as the potter's wheel

The souls of Jonathan and David were knit together, tied together in
the bundle of life (1 Samuel 18:1). They were wrapped up in God,
tucked in, as the body is in the bed clothes. We, in Jesus Christ, are

like that...vine and branch, root and shoot, sheep and shepherd, stones and corner stone. What a relationship! What a consolation! What considered condescension on the part of God!

There is a firm of Wine Distillers in the City of Leeds where cheap wines are mixed with good wines and blended until an acceptable wine is produced. Through association with Jesus, that which was so ordinary can become glorious, fit for a King's Table. We can become so like Him and He so like us, that Judas has to kiss Him to mark Him out among His brethren.

Jesus enters into every area and fills it with His new nature, via a new birth. We are full, never empty, never lonely, never alone. We are never left as a scarecrow is left in the middle of a field, nor forsaken as a plague. We are loved with an everlasting love, embraced as the Prodigal son.

Loneliness can be lost in the friendship of faith

There is a greater emphasis in the Greek language than in the English translation..."I will never, never, never, never, never leave you" (Hebrews 13:5). Tied with so many knots, sealed with so many seals. The word "never" is stronger in the original — repeat it to perfection. I will surround you on every side, even as every side of the bird is covered with feathers and all parts of your body are covered with skin, I will be with you in such a fulness as this. There are War Memorials where flames of remembrance are lit, ever to burn. There are Books of Remembrance where names are written in them forever. Can I not have stamped on my relationship with Jesus Christ "Forever"? I will never fail you and I will never forsake you. The Lord is my helper. I will not be afraid. What can man do to me? (Hebrews 13:6).

God means to get us where He wants us to be. In Hebrews 6:20 there is a lovely metaphor of a ship outside the port. It is in the fog and it is in the "offing", it cannot get to where it wants to be. A little ship goes out to it, a "forerunner". It takes a rope from the ship, comes out of the harbour through the mist and storm, and leads the large ship back into port. The larger ship is towed by the smaller. Jesus is the Forerunner. It doesn't matter on which desert island life leaves us, the Forerunner will come to us and draw us into those safer waters, the haven which has been designed for us. We who have been brought out will be brought up closer to Jesus Christ. There is no need to be the only pebble on the beach, the only star in the sky. Like Job, you can be tried as gold from the crucible to shine and share all the riches of His grace and glory. Our life is Christ and Christ is our life. "For me to live is Christ and to die is gain." I live, speak, eat, think and act Jesus Christ, my lifelong Companion.

Then, I awoke. I had dreamed it all during my time of drifting between the hands of my wife and the Hands of God. Yet my dream was a reality, and I have my Bible to prove it! The dream has gone, but the thoughts linger on. If I am ever tempted now to be lonely, I think on these things.

CHAPTER
10

The Diversity of Healings in the Adversity of Suffering

There are diversities of operations, but it is the same God which works all in all. (1 Corinthians 12:3-6)

God never meets the same need in the same way. He is a God of variety, that is why grace is described as being manifold — multi coloured. As we look back over this book, we have seen the different aspects of suffering, and yet, there has been as many ways for God to help, as there has been needs. God never uses a rubber stamp as He meets your requirements. Even the tailor or seamstress will tell you that we all have differing measurements and requirements. As there were a number of rivers flowing out of the Garden Of Eden, so there are a number of ministries which will help you in your suffering. That is why the months of the year provide differently in Nature. Arriving from many angles, some of them acute, God meets the suffering in the best possible way, through the best possible means available at the time. Every time God meets with you, it is always tied to his tender will. Every time God says, I will, he is married to your suffering. He may not do it in your time, or using the method you desire, but when he does, everything is beautiful in its own time.

There are many paths travelling from the Cross of Christ, and each path is paved with ointments of healing qualities. These paths run from chapter one to chapter ten of this book, through sickness and health, through all manner of suffering, through loneliness, providing patience, through understanding, on to grace and glory. They provide the strength we require in weakness, they heal our bruisings, and dispel our loneliness.

142

✳   ✳   ✳

For many people, the Gifts of the Spirit will only be seen in what are termed miraculous operations. They are the Gifts of Power, Miracles, Signs and Wonders yet in 1 Corinthians 12:28 when Paul is concluding his argument, likening different gifts to the parts of the body, he uses the words Governments, Administrations, Surrounded by Miracles and Speaking in Other Tongues. Helps are placed next to healings proving that many supposedly natural happenings have God as their source and guide into healing. We seek to take physical healing and place it on one side as if that is all there is to healings and giftings, 1 Corinthians 12:28, first, secondly and thirdly, and there is no apportioning of the gift to any place. There is no A to Z list of importance or function once you move from the Apostle, Prophet and Teacher. In Romans the same applies. Chapter 12:6,7 — teaching is included alongside Prophecy, Giving and Ruling, along with Mercy, are there as part of that which the Spirit of God operates through. Large or small they are God orientated.

God has an abundance when it comes to the gift of healing. He has so many channels He uses, even as the rivers which ran out of the Garden of Eden and parted into four heads, each containing something precious (Genesis 2:10). There are those who think that healing of body soul and spirit can only come one way, but the ways of God are unable to be counted. Many operations, but the same Lord over all. Diversity of Gifts but the same Spirit. Differences of Administration, but the same Lord.

The brand name matters when we deal with healing. The terms Lord, God or Spirit will determine the content and the outcome.

The manner in which I receive my healing may not be the same as another, and I must be mature enough to accept this. There is no scriptural pattern or mould which demands that we all come through it, no door marked "healings".

It was believed, after a serious car accident, that a clot of blood had gone to my brain. I was subject to rolling eyes and fits, and the consent form for an operation was being prepared for my wife to sign. Suddenly it was decided that the clot had disappeared and there would be no need to operate. God had answered the prayers of those who had been praying for me! Little by little I recovered fully and gave God all the glory and thanks. Today, many years later, I am still well and strong.

Let us consider the different forms of healing.

There is divine healing

When a miracle takes place it can only be attributed to Divine intervention. Let us please move away from the idea that someone must always lay hands on us, we must buy their videos or attend great Crusades. Many a person has died clutching a glossy magazine! Having hands laid on us or being anointed with oil can be a method which God uses, but it is not the only one. Scriptures state that we can be anointed with oil and prayed for. There is no mention of the laying on of hands. It is "praying over him" (James 5:14) — and it has to be a prayer of faith.

There is an instance in the Word of God where King Hezekiah was told to take a lump of figs and place them on the troubled area. The ingredients of the figs, the healing qualities, were applied and God, in His kindness and mercy, passed through those figs, using them as fingers of healing and rays of light (2 Kings 20:7). God did care a fig!

Elisha, to raise a young child from the dead, stretched himself eye to eye and mouth to mouth on the child, and the child was restored fully (2 Kings 4:34).

At the bitter waters of Marah a piece of wood was thrown into the waters and they were healed to become sweet tasting (Exodus 15:25), such as could have been brought to the Wedding at Cana of Galilee.

A man thrown into the grave of Elisha (2 Kings 13:21) bounced back out!

It poses the question — Whose faith created these miracles?

All healings are not physical

Hebrews 11 gives a list of diversity of miracles created by faith — the mouths of the lions were stopped; Hebrew lads who would not eat the King's meat were just as fat as the ones who did! Noah, and how he built the Ark. I have noted that there is not one miracle of healing in Hebrews Chapter 11, they are all acts of faith without physical healings. Jesus mixed His spit with dust and told a man to apply it to his eyes — and he received his sight. Others were healed from leprosy as they walked along, and on other occasions Jesus spoke soft words to bring healing and health into sick bodies. At the grave of Lazarus in John 11:43 He commanded Lazarus to come forth. Some He touched, others He spoke to, and with others He sent the Word ahead, like some herald of God. The shadow of Peter moving along the streets in the midday sun suddenly and dramatically became the vehicle of healing for those who were sick (Acts 5:15). Shadow led to substance. People who were dead and thereby had no faith, were raised from the dead. The mind cannot take this in, but faith facilitates it all. Peter's shadow was even able to deal with unclean spirits!

There are special healings

Paul was used to bring special miracles to early believers — his handkerchiefs were placed on the sick (Acts 19:12). These pieces of cloth so often used to dry tears or wipe sweaty brows were used by God to mop up sickness and to drive out evil spirits without a word being spoken.

There is a text which speaks of the Power of the Lord being present to heal — Luke 5:17. A Presence ready to help in healing.

There are instances where God healed independently of anything which was done or said or even believed. God could have given the women coming to the tomb the strength to roll the stone away, but He chose to send angels and caused an earthquake to do it for them (Matthew 28:2). The power, personality and the purposes of Christ were established in many and various ways.

We believe in healings which are substantiated

I believe in Divine healing but it has to be the real thing and not something suggested, psychosomatic, not auto-suggestion. Not, "I feel a little better, I can now walk two steps where before it was only one." It certainly must not be "If you send me money God will heal you". Gehazi suffered for that sin in the Old Testament — 2 Kings 5:25-27.

I do not have all the answers. If I did, I would not be writing this book, I would simply be praying for the sick and seeing everyone instantly healed, but it does not always happen that way and we have to be realistic. If healing has not taken place, then do not make up a case for God that it has happened. Let the evidence of the blind receiving their sight be in the blind actually seeing, the lame walking, the deaf hearing, the Aids victim being declared healed by the medical profession. God does not need me as a prop for the work He is going to do. I don't have to insist that a horse is a horse, let it be what it is! I do not have to argue that a miracle is a miracle if it is a mirage!

My problem with Divine healing is not those who are healed, it is with those who are not healed. Must they be rejected, cast on one side? Must they be told they have no faith? What about the faith of the Evangelist: Is that always operating? Has he that particular Gift?

The Will of God and healings

There has to be the allowance of the Will of God in every situation. Every case must be dealt with on its own merits. I want to know about the old people in our Churches whose bodies begin to wear out, what about those who believe and yet who do not receive? Everyone who dies does so through a measure of sickness, some part of the body has failed them. What about those who have continued to be sick and yet, because of that sickness, have given light and love to others which they would never have possessed had it not been for their affliction? Without naming names there are many who are writing, singing, preaching, despite their afflictions! Shall not the Judge of the earth do right? (Genesis 18:25). Is not the wrath of God kinder than the love of men? Yes! Every time!

There were many in the Old and the New Testament who were not healed, who were still sick even after associating with Peter, Paul and John. 2 Timothy 4:20..."Trophimus have I left at Miletum, sick". Paul too, according to the N.I.V. was a sick person, Galatians 4:13. James, who wrote the Epistle, had the nickname of "Camel's knees" because of their condition and his much praying! Surely God could have healed him?

We are told to:

> *"lay hands on the sick and they shall recover"* (Mark 16:18)

We are instructed to pray the prayer of faith. We are directed to anoint with oil. If two shall be agreed on earth as touching anything connected with God's Kingdom it shall be done (Matthew 18:19). The effectual fervent prayers of a righteous man avail much (James 5:16). They procure the promise.

Healing has many slaves

We must get away from the idea that God only heals through the hands of an Evangelist. It can happen like that, and no doubt you have heard stories of healings when no human instrument was used. Smith Wigglesworth[1], one of the early Pentecostal pioneers, went to Sweden where the Law forbade him to lay hands on the sick. He prayed from the platform and scores were healed! He would ask them to raise their hands and the first one who did so would be healed! It happened! God's methods are not always the methods of men. One man in Wakefield was told by God to visit a Hospital Chapel and that morning he would be healed. Another, in a wheelchair for many years, was told the day she would be healed as the hands of a new convert were laid upon her. God has many "evangelists" who never enter a pulpit!

There is healing within the Body of Christ

There is such a thing as Body Ministry, not everyone laying hands on everyone else, but God has set some in the Church with ministry gifts — healings, miracles, signs and wonders (Mark 16:17; 1 Corinthians 12:28). Every part of your body has some part to play and gifts are not simply deposited in the Pastor, Teacher or

Evangelist, but in each member of the Body — 1 Corinthians 12 — as God divides "severally" as He wills (1 Corinthians 12:11). Mark 16:16 - 18...healing can be a confirmation of ourselves as believers. A miracle confirms the words of God. He has stamped His Word with a miracle, and authenticates it. The preached word was confirmed. Different parts of the body, not just the head, assist with healing — eyes to see, hands to apply, nerves to feel, emotion to move with compassion, flesh to stick together in a natural way. So it should be spiritually also. Not just an Evangelist has the gift of healing, a man can be an Apostle and have miracles attending his ministry, or a Pastor and the same should apply. A person exercising that gift of the Holy Spirit can be an expression of the outshining of that Spirit, a miracle in what he gives and how it meets the need. Each can be used by God. 1 Corinthians 7:7...Every man has his proper gift. There are agencies within the Church which need loosing so that others might be set free.

When Jesus was transfigured in Matthew 17:2 — there was a demon-possessed boy in the valley and the transfiguration of Jesus was not completed until that boy was delivered. The transfiguration of Jesus will not be completed until the unemployed are employed, until the poor are fed, the homeless housed, until we all dwell together in peace. We can play a part in this as we allow God to use our giftings. He will make provision and His own choices as the Sovereign Lord as to what shall and shall not be. We are told that David, after he had served the will of God, fell on sleep. The Greek for *"will"* is plural, *"wills"* (Acts 13:36). Each miracled ministry, miracle mission, each miracle, is one of the wills of God for our generation and each manifestation is for the glorification of Jesus. It is a display of the will of God. The vehicle which brings the healing does not matter, the fact that God does heal is sufficient.

There are pastoral healings

The Minister's ministry of the miraculous should make him the Master of all trades and the Jack of none. He should be gentle, kind, understanding and beautiful, placing gems of true worth into vessels of clay. Only Heaven will fully reveal all the interventions the local

Pastor accomplishes. He prays, visits, blesses, preaches the word and prays for the sick, many times with great results, yet not making headline news. He tends his flock and, by his presence and wise words ministers healing to them. He visits those in divorce, disease, desperate straits, the lonely, the family arguments, the son who has left home, the people who feel threatened, the homeless, the bereaved and the fearful. With what diverse pains they come, but with what joy they leave! There is that which withholds and tends to poverty, there is that which scatters and increases. It is not an easy battle, it is uphill all the way — but it is UP!

The nature of pastoral healings is difficult. Luke 1:2 — *"Ministers"* meaning *"under rowers"*. It is difficult to row a boat, particularly when the sea is stormy, the night is long and you have caught nothing. Reflecting the love of Christ the Minister is one who acts under the direction, promptings of another. The word "Minister" means sometimes, "one who has dust on his feet", or a person who performs public duties at his own expense. He is a miracle worker in the truest sense of the word, in the Church and in the world at large. It is a pity that occasionally, due to overwork and underpay, the local Minister in his healing exercise has had to surrender much of his work to psychiatrist, psychologist and social worker!

God still ministers healing and help, even through those who are non-believers..."Other sheep have I which are not of this fold" (John 10:16). If God could raise up ungodly Pharaoh then I can believe that He still does it today to bring glory to His Name.

Some helps can be a back door into the Church and to God. If that is so, then so be it. As long as the mountain peaks in the same sky and we see people clothed and in their right minds, seated at the feet of Jesus (Luke 8:35), that is the most important fact. They that are for us are not against us.

There are medical healings

I thank God for the profession which does so much to alleviate pain and suffering by the use of medicine. Technology has been a mighty instrument in healing and health. Every chemist's shop can be part of the healing process. Doctors have God-given abilities and, if they choose not to Name the Maker, then that is to their folly. The very medicines they prescribe come from God's earth! All can be traced back to the Hand of God Who first created man and gave him a brain with which to diagnose! Thank God for those nurses who gather each morning for prayer, for those doctors and surgeons who pray before they act — accomplishing all that they do in the Name of God. There is healing in the hands of the doctors. Every nursery, clinic, surgery and hospital should be a Bethesda "House of Mercy".

There are scientific healings

Radium has helped so many! The laser technology has done so much good. All the great discoveries made during the last century are all God given and God blessed, a form of healing administered in another way. Whether hand-shaped, bottle-shaped, pill-shaped or liquid they are still expressions of the gifts of God to the whole of mankind. It is not the container, but the content that counts. Those who are working at this present time to discover a cure for AIDS, may God help them, and that right early! Science makes discoveries for the medical world to apply — when Eddystone asked God to help him to make a discovery, he said, "God said, alright! Get to work!" Who can doubt the great healing qualities of Florence Nightingale, Louis Pasteur, James Simpson and his discovery of chloroform, the field of antibiotics with Alexander Fleming, Marie Curie and radium, Christian Barnard's heart transplants...there are so many lesser discoveries also which we take so much for granted. God placed them all there in the beginning, that they might be discovered. No longer do we have to take alcohol or bite on the bullet whilst we are operated on — if the shock didn't kill us the bacteria would!

There are time healings

Some things, if little attention is given, will over a period of time result in healing. There is a time for healing. Time acts as a needle stitching together that which has been torn apart. The run down is wound back up, the worn parts are refurbished, the bent becomes straight. Mental breakdowns, nervous disorders, many times it is a matter of time which works as a medicine, a healer of frayed nerve ends. Time puts us back together again, slowly, where we belong. Time is a great healer and, like the rising of the sun, will not be hurried. Father Time and Mother Nature form a marvellous partnership and have a wonderful dispensing chemist, working together to help humanity. What Mother Nature cannot lift, Father Time takes hold of. When Mother Nature leaves bleeding and dying, then Father Time takes and helps into healing. Time is on your side, all who take time will recover with time.

There are prayer healings

When we come to God in prayer there is a promise for us. *"Be still and know that I am God"* (Psalm 46:10). *"Let go and let God."* The word of God to Moses concerning Israel — *"Tell them to stand still"...*"Tell them to go forward"* (Exodus 14:15). To Elijah *"Show Thyself"*, *"Hide Thyself"* (1 Kings 17:3; 18:1). Isaiah 40:31, *"They that wait upon the Lord shall renew their strength."* The sand becomes rock, the clay becomes steel. Their weakness for His strength. There is an impartation of the life of the Spirit of God in us as we wait on Him. We have to rest on Christ and in prayer until God makes all our bed in sickness. We wait for Him to work — "They serve who only stand and wait". When the dust finally settles, there is Adam reformed in it and ready! Listen to the advice of Jesus "Come ye apart and rest a while". If you do not come apart then you will fall apart, and all the king's horses and all the king's men will not be able to put you together again!

As we pray, quietness and peace become the order of the day. There is a hush in the corridor of life, God's Holy quietness begins to descend. As we pray we open up the avenues of peace. The tiredness, the fret and the threat are harnessed and brought under the control of God. Men should not "faint". Psalm 55:22. *"Cast thy burden upon the Lord."* Burden — gift. God turns burdens into gifts. Prayer sees a burden converted into something else, not to be borne, but to be used as a gift. Let troubles, like winds, drive us as small ships into a quiet bay until the storms lessen and we are made ready for future activities.

There are food healings

Healthy staple diet has as much to do with healing as anything else. There are certain vitamins needed to keep the body alive and well. The body is dying every day, certain cells have died whilst you have been reading this! Provisions are made in food for the brightness of the eye and the fairness of the skin. Lack food and you will lack health, vital stamina will be missing.

There are rest healings

There are moments of rest which count for a cure for the hours of running, rushing, tripping, falling and worrying...times when it is good to take the floor off your feet! The anchors need lowering to hold us from drifting onto the rocks perilously close to sand banks.

Sleep and rest are beautiful, for they provide the things that life has snatched from us, bringing us back into line and shape. Sometimes we need to be placed on our backs to make us look up and reach for things in the sky, rather than those on the earth.

As Christians we need to maintain our composure, and health needs healthy inactivity to promote it and to strengthen. Some need more rest than others.

David trusted in the Lord. The margin of the King James, Psalm 22:8, says, *"He rolled himself on to the Lord". "Lay on the Lord as on a bed!"* Relax on God as you would on a bed to sleep. When a carpet is rolled onto a floor the tread is softer, lighter, easier. There is a healing that is released into the human system as we rest. The cogitations of the heart are caressed with the kisses of rest. Nothing will care for your physical frame more than rest.

When Martin Luther could not rest because of the challenge of meeting with the dignitaries, his wife said to him, "Martin, didn't God look after the world before you came into it?" "Yes." "Don't you think the Almighty can look after it whilst you sleep then?" His chagrin defeated, he turned over and went soundly to sleep!

Each person needs to bring the broken cups and plates to the potter, bring the jangled nerves and place them at the feet of Christ. We live in Him and we sleep in Him, we rest in Him and we rise in Him. Sit with Mary! Discover that all those who came and sat at the feet of Jesus went away transformed. To rest awhile in His Presence means we will not come apart, we can recharge the batteries, refill the bucket. David's harp "refreshed" Saul (1 Samuel 16:23). Paul had those who refreshed him (2 Timothy 1:16). Sometimes the life is knocked out of us, it is uphill all the way, we are left panting and gasping for breath — Rest, until the Holy Spirit breathes again upon us with the freshness of Heaven. Times of refreshing from the Presence of the Lord (Acts 3:19).

There are herbal healings

Every plant, root, nut, leaf and stalk is given for the good of mankind. God, through Mother Nature, plants shrubs all around us to act as some stockade for our health and healing. Man commenced life among plants in a garden. The juices are there to be extracted and to put back those things which life takes out of us. They act and react on our behalf. Jesus told the Parable of the Sower and the Seed (Matthew 13:18-23). One plant withered because it lacked moisture (Luke 8:6). "Moisture" is a normal medical word for the fluids of the body, when they have dried up.

In the Book of Revelation (Revelations 22:2) we read of a tree with leaves for the healing of the nations.

Many modern medicines find their sources in plant life. Whatever method brings relief all can be used and all can bring health flowing back into our bodies. Herbs contain so many healing properties. Wood-sorrel is shaped like a heart, and is useful as a cordial. Liverwort is used by those suffering with liver complaints. The herb known as celandine has yellow juice and is used for jaundice. Herb-dragon, which is speckled like a dragon used to be used for serpent bites and stings.

Heaven will be the fullness of healing

It is sad to think that there is so much medicine and yet so many people who are still sick. There is a day and place where there is no sickness, no night, no sorrows, no tears. When a patient is healed God is breaking no laws, He simply adds another Law, another dimension into the Laws which we know, it is as if another light is being shone into what is a dark place. Natural law says that if a sickness is terminal, then you will die. God is able to bring another law into operation which is able to result in healing! Whatever is introduced, if it brings relief, if it eases pain, if it straightens the leg, focuses the eye, then God be praised! I see God at work in all forms of healing...other than the occult, of course! When sickness raises its ugly head then we need that which will help us to bring, in life and in death, glory to God. Many words in the Bible are used for sickness. Sickness is a disorder. Medicine and healing bring order, and a new order at that! It is a wasting away, a setting like the sun as if the day has reached its end, a running out of water from a cracked or broken vessel, it is to be unwell, to be weak, sickly, frail, without strength, to be seized and held captive. I have found One Who has paid the ransom — Jesus Christ! I must accept every form of healing into my sore and my sickness. God says, "I am the God Who heals you" (Exodus 15:26).

Healing like suffering challenges and changes us all

When we are healed we are well and strong again — sometimes after prayer, other times having been anointed with oil, or because of medicines, tablets, herbs, changes of climate — all are part of God's dispensary. When we are healed we are repaired, that which has been broken is mended, that torn apart is stitched. The hollow is filled with good things. We have been made thoroughly sound. As Jesus said to the Man of Gadara, "Go and tell what great things God has done for you" (Luke 8:39). Lord, I believe, help thou mine unbelief! (Mark 9:24). God has many witnesses and some of them are as those back from the dead. They appear in another form. They are changed for the better. There are those who will question if it is really him, he looks so well and strong! The healing is so full. Like the blind man in John 9:9 — it looks like him!

All who are healed have been given remedies from the Hand of God. The Hand of good which, when opened, satisfies the desire of every living thing (Psalm 145:16). As Job says, "Shall we not receive good and evil from the hand of the Lord?" (Job 2:10). It is still the hand of the Lord, despite being in a bottle or tasting like cod liver oil! Healing is that which raises us up and strengthens us. Luke 9:11, "He healed all those who had need of healing." He gave them an "attendance", the meaning of healing, which would minister to their needs, the nurse who waited on them until they were healed. How good is the God we adore! Soundness, peace, safety, assurance, well-being are all included in healing.

The healing itself is the way of giving thanks to God for what has been accomplished. May we join with others in offering God thanks that He has brought us through sickness and into health. In the healthy times I will praise Him and in the sick times I will worship Him. By life or by death, may Christ be magnified in my body (Philippians 1:20).

NOTE

1. Smith Wigglesworth, an early Pentecostal evangelist, used to pray for the sick. *Apostle of Faith*, Stanley H. Frodsham (Gospel Publishing House, Springfield, Missouri, America), p.107.

BIBLIOGRAPHY

A.S.V., Authorised Standard Version
Barclay, W.,
Bunyan, John, *The Pilgrim's Progress*,
Clarke, Adam
Eddystone,
Eunice, A.,
Gill, Dr. John,
Goodspeed,
Hackett,
Idahosa, Benson, *Fire in his Bones*,
Jones, Stanley,
King James Version
Living Bible, The
Moffat,
Moody, D.L.,
Morgan, G.C.,
N.I.V., New International Version.
Philips, J.B.,
R.S.V.,
Strong, Dr.,
Tyndale,
Varah, Rev Chad,
Wigglesworth, Smith,